# EARLY DILMUN SEALS
# FROM SAAR

*With the compliments of*

London–Bahrain Archaeological Expedition:
Saar Excavation Reports II

# EARLY
# DILMUN
# SEALS
## FROM SAAR

Art and Commerce in Bronze Age Bahrain

by

## Harriet Crawford

## ARCHAEOLOGY INTERNATIONAL

in association with

London–Bahrain Archaeological Expedition
Ministry of Cabinet Affairs and Information, State of Bahrain
Institute of Archaeology, University College London

First published in 2001 by
Archaeology International
Upper House, Stoke Saint Milborough
Ludlow SY8 2EJ
Tel: 044 (1)584 823303 Fax: 044 (1)584 823389
E-mail: enquiries@archaeology-international.co.uk

©

Text: HEW Crawford; Graphics: London-Bahrain Archaeological
Expedition (2001)

Published in Great Britain

**British Library Cataloguing in Publication Data**
Crawford, Harriet
Early Dilmun Seals from Saar: Art & Commerce in Bronze Age Bahrain
1. Title
939.4'9
ISBN 0-9539561-0-5

# Contents

# Foreword

Recent archaeological exploration and allied research have provided us with a wealth of new information about many aspects of the Dilmun culture. Results of this work suggest that we must reconsider our views on many aspects of early Bahrain. The study of seals and sealings in particular provides a major opportunity for shedding light on social and economic aspects of Dilmun and I am confident that it is also the key to a better understanding of the origin and development of this unique civilization.

This volume presents the major collection of seals and sealings found by the London-Bahrain Archaeological Expedition at Saar, dating to the early second millennium BC.

The Dilmun settlement and the temple found at this site constitute the principle archaeological discovery on Bahrain during the past decade. Dr Harriet Crawford has given the subject careful treatment, using an easy and fluent style that meets the needs of specialists and researchers in this field. This work is, without doubt, an important and worthy addition to the study of Dilmun.

**Mohammed Ebrahim Al-Mottawa**
*Minister of Cabinet Affairs and Information*
*State of Bahrain*

# Acknowledgements

This is the second volume in the final publications of the excavations carried out by the London–Bahrain Archaeological Expedition at the site of Saar, on the main island of Bahrain, between 1990 and 1999. This work was only possible because of the generous support of a great number of people. First and foremost, we acknowledge the help of the Ministry of Cabinet Affairs and Information, and would like to thank particularly HE Mohammed Al-Motawa, Minister of Cabinet Affairs and Information, Dr Abdullah Yateem, Assistant Under-Secretary for Culture, Shaikha Nayla bin Ali Al-Khalifa, Director of Archaeology and Heritage, and Mr Khalid Al-Sindi, Superintendent of Archaeology, who has a great fund of information on the seals of the Early Dilmun Period.

We also gratefully acknowledge the generous financial support and help-in-kind given to the Saar Project between 1995 and 2000 by the following companies: ABN Amro, African & Eastern, Airmech, Al Ahli Commercial Bank, Aluminium Bahrain, American Women's Association, Arab Banking Corporation, Arabian Exhibition Management, Bahrain Airport Services, Bahrain Kuwait Insurance Company, Bahrain National Holding, Bahrain Petroleum Company, Banagas, Bank of Bahrain and Kuwait, Banque Nationale de Paris, Bahrain Maritime & Mercantile International, Bahrain Technical & Trading Company, Basrec, Batelco, The British Bank, The British Council, Budget Rent-A-Car, Business International, Cable & Wireless, Caltex Bahrain, Citibank, Clifford Chance, Crown Worldwide Movers, Diplomat Hotel, Ernst & Young, Flemings, Grindlays Bahrain Bank, Gulf Colour Laboratories, Gulf Daily News, Gulf Petrochemical Industries Company, Hasan Mansouri Group, Inchcape, Intercol Group, Investcorp, Jashanmals, Kodak Near East, KPMG Fakhro, Linacre Associates, Mohammed Jalal & Sons, Nass Scafform, Philip Morris, Serco-IAL, Standard Chartered Bank, Unitag, United Gulf Bank, United Insurance Company, and Yateem Brothers.

We are also grateful for the major support for the publication of this book that we have received from the Ministry of Cabinet Affairs & Information, and from Arab Banking Corporation, Al Ahli Bank, Aluminium Bahrain, Batelco, Bahrain International Bank, Caltex Bahrain, Dilmun Investments and Philip Morris.

My personal thanks go especially to Jane Moon and Robert Killick who suggested that I write this book and who helped me with advice at every stage of its production. Any remaining errors are entirely my responsibility. My warmest thanks also go to Tessa Rickards who drew the impressions of the seals themselves and with whom I spent much time trying to understand the more abstruse aspects of the designs! I am also grateful to Dr Lamia Al Gailani-Werr for looking at an early draft of the introduction.

**Harriet Crawford**
*September 2000*

# 1 Introduction

The archaeology of the Arabian Gulf has been transformed in the last twenty years by an explosion of new information. There has been a growing awareness in the Gulf itself and in the rest of the world of the importance of its heritage. This is attributable to a number of factors: to an emergent sense of national identity, to changing economic circumstances, which are forcing formerly oil-rich nations to look to alternative means of generating income, such as tourism, and to the political situation in the Middle East. Recent conflicts have made access to countries such as Iraq and Iran impossible for many scholars, so focussing research on more welcoming regions. Areas such as the Gulf were once regarded as peripheral to the so-called High Civilizations of Egypt and Mesopotamia, and it is only now, as a result of the new data

produced by intensified research, that their importance is being recognised. The Gulf is a natural corridor, linking cultures and continents as far apart as Africa, Asia, and India, and the people who lived there in prehistoric times blended many elements to produce a way of life which was well-suited to a difficult environment, and whose material culture had its own distinctive character.

One of the major powers in the Gulf in the late third and early second millennia BC was known in the cuneiform record as Dilmun, a land with the dual character of a mythological country which was the home of the Sumerian Noah, Ziusudra, and a thriving commercial centre. Texts and archaeology together show that by the late third millennium BC the real Dilmun was centred on the island of Bahrain (Potts 1990, p. 181). Recently, thanks to work carried out by scholars from Bahrain and from many other countries, the real Dilmun has begun to emerge from the mists of mythology and can now take its place as a vital entrepot in the network of trade routes which criss-crossed the ancient Near East at this period.

A great deal of information is available on the international trade which underpinned the economy of Dilmun, thanks largely to the cuneiform texts found in Mesopotamia. (For summaries see Potts 1990, Crawford 1998a.) The picture painted by the texts is also supported by the archaeological evidence from the Bahrain Islands. Their most notable archaeological features in the nineteenth century AD, when the first European visitors recorded their impressions of the island, were the great fields of burial mounds. Sadly, these have been extensively robbed over the centuries, but where their contents survive, they paint the same picture of a country with wide ranging contacts. The so-called Royal Graves at A'ali in particular yielded tantalising remains of a sophisticated material culture using a wide range of imported goods and

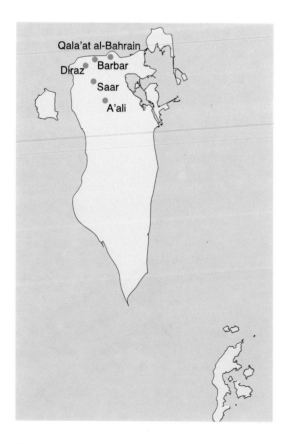

**Fig. 1 Major Early Dilmun sites in Bahrain.**

materials, which included fragments of ivory carvings from pieces of furniture as well as gold jewellery and copper weapons (Reade & Burleigh 1978).

The first extensive modern archaeological investigations of Bahrain produced important evidence on the indigenous culture of the islands, and were undertaken almost fifty years ago by Danish teams under Professor Glob, Professor Mortensen and Geoffrey Bibby (Bibby 1972) at Qala'at al-Bahrain, a large stratified tell site on the north coast of the main Bahrain island. The site apparently covered about 15 ha in the so-called Early Dilmun period, at around 2000 BC (Højlund 2000, p. 60), but much of the early material is deeply stratified under later deposits, making access difficult. In spite of

this, the Danish expedition was able to establish a stratified sequence of pottery from the mid-third millennium BC to the Hellenistic period and to identify a short length of the early second millennium BC city wall, with some adjacent buildings (Højlund & Andersen 1994). More recently work has continued at the site under a French team, which has been exploring the later second millennium levels. Professor Mortensen, in a second Danish project, uncovered a temple of approximately the same date as the city wall at Barbar, a village about 3 km to the south-west of Qala'at al-Bahrain which gave further indications of the prosperity of the period and of the technical skills of the builders (Mortensen 1986, Andersen 1986). Imported objects

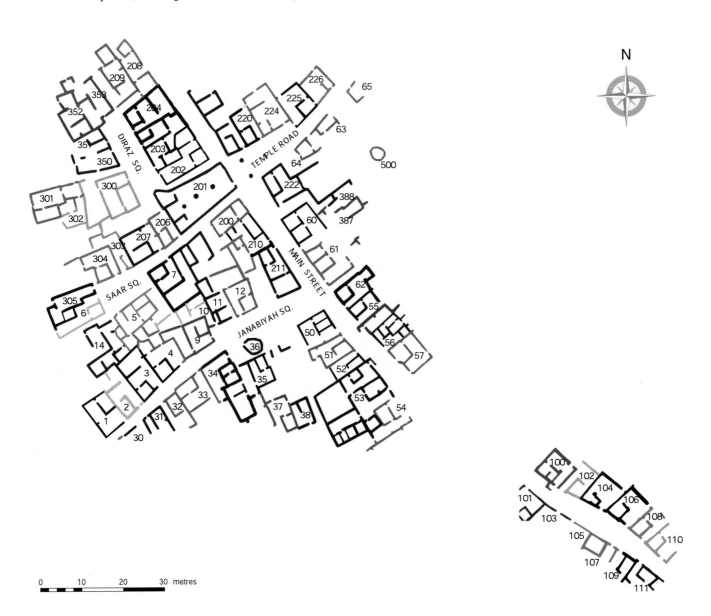

**Fig. 2 Schematic plan of Saar settlement.**

**Fig. 3 The Saar Temple and adjacent buildings.**

found in the temple, as well as objects made of imported materials, reinforced the image of Dilmun as an important trading nation.

What was missing from the emerging picture of Dilmun, the trading nation, was detailed information on the domestic economy and social structure of the island in the Early Dilmun period, information on how local people actually lived and on how their society was organised.

The London–Bahrain Archaeological Expedition (LBAE) was set up in 1989 to begin the work of filling this gap in our knowledge by identifying and excavating a smaller settlement site of the period.[1]

The site of Saar in the north-west of the island was chosen (Fig. 1), because initial work by a joint Bahraini–Jordanian team in the 1980s had established the presence there of extensive remains of an essentially single-period Early Dilmun site covering about 2.5 ha. This lay immediately under the surface, with no overburden, and appeared relatively undisturbed. The earlier work had been

suspended, but permission was granted for the LBAE to start work there again in the spring of 1990, since when ten seasons of excavation have taken place.[2]

The site lies on a north-south limestone ridge on which stood an extensive mound field composed of thousands of burial mounds, now largely destroyed, and at least two subterranean burial complexes (Ibrahim 1982 and Mughal 1983). To the east of the ridge is an area rich in springs, now used as a date garden. A well belonging to the ancient settlement also lay to the east. Today the coast is about 3 km to the west and about 7 km to the east of Saar, but geological maps of the area indicate that *sabkha*, or compacted sand, on the east comes within 3 km of the site and a tongue of sea reached much closer to the ridge within living memory. It seems likely that this was also the case in the early second millennium BC and there may well have been a sheltered anchorage below the site on this side.

**1.** The directors of the expedition were Robert Killick and Jane Moon, and the author, who retired as a director after five years.

**2.** Permission was granted by the Ministry of Information, State of Bahrain, without whose constant support and encouragement the work of the Expedition would not have been possible. Preliminary reports on the work have appeared as follows: Killick at al. 1991, Crawford 1993, Woodburn & Crawford 1994, Moon et al. 1995, Moon & Killick 1995, and Killick et al. 1997.

The importance of the sea to the domestic economy of the settlement was immediately obvious. Fish and shellfish seem to have been the major source of protein and their remains include many of both the inland and deep-water species found in the waters around Bahrain today. Evidence for agriculture was also recovered, but unfortunately preservation of carbonised plant remains at Saar was poor. However, there is evidence for the presence of small amounts of wheat and barley, together with a little chaff, and there are large numbers of quernstones and rubbers which were probably used for processing plants for human consumption. Dates were eaten in quantity, and one flax seed was also recovered (de Moulins 1997). Sheep, goat and cattle were the main domesticates, and although a few wild animal bones were found, hunting does not seem to have made a significant contribution to the domestic economy.

The settlement, of which it is estimated that around 75% has now been explored, has four main chronological levels, of which the first, Level 1, was only reached in a number of deep soundings.[3] These indicated that the settlement was much smaller than the one we see today.

There was no temple, and the roads did not run on their present alignments. It dates to the late third millennium BC. In Level II there was a major reconstruction and enlargement of the settlement; the present road system was put in place, the temple was built, and the buildings covered approximately the area we see today. In this period the temple dominated the settlement, standing on the highest point at an elevation of around 12 m at the junction of two major roads, called by the excavators 'Main Street' and 'Temple Road' (Fig. 2). The temple is isolated from the other buildings by two smaller alleys which run north and south of it.

In Level II, the temple (Crawford et al. 1997) was built of the same local stone as the other buildings, held together with gypsum mortar, and the walls were originally heavily plastered both inside and out. It is trapezoidal in shape, 17.5 m long, with a curious bulge in the exterior wall in the northern corner which formed a separate small room, apparently used for storage. A second storage area lay adjacent to it to the south. In the main room, the roof was supported on three centrally placed pillars, two square ones, and a third round one at the eastern end, where a

**Fig. 4 Building 100 towards the south-eastern edge of the settlement.**

**Fig. 5 A standard oven. Thirty five of this type were found at Saar.**

**Fig. 6 A storage jar set into the floor of a house (2694:01. Diam. of vessel 38 cm).**

**Fig. 7 Imported agate bead (1773:01; height 3.3 cm).**

single, rather narrow door gives access to the building. There was an altar on the south wall, decorated with a semicircular plastered feature at the back, the interpretation of which has aroused much interest. It has been suggested that the feature may be a schematic rendering of bulls' horns, or that it may represent the crescent moon. There is evidence for burnt offerings of fish and vegetable matter having been made on the altar. A platform was built against the east wall, and a bench and low step stood against the north wall at right angles to the platform. All these features are very finely plastered and on the top of the platform the imprint of a rectangular base is still preserved. Outside the building, in the open area to the east, were five circular emplacements.

West of Main Street, and south of the temple, parallel to the alleys on either side of it, is a smaller road leading up to the limestone ridge to the west. East of Main Street, two more small roads have been identified, leading eastwards, parallel to Temple Road, towards a well. The smaller roads divide up the buildings in the centre of the settlement into blocks of not more than four or five units. Main Street itself begins at the northern edge of the settlement and then runs south from the temple for about 200 m before entering a modern garden and becoming impossible to trace.

The settlement seems to have had a surprisingly regular layout, which may be the result of some sort of overall plan, rather than of organic growth, although the plan visible today has seen a number of alterations during the life of the settlement. The main street roughly bisects the settlement, while Temple Road is oriented at right angles to it, and towards the façade of the temple itself. The alleys run off the main road at fairly regular intervals, and in one instance at least four buildings, 202–205, share an unbroken back-wall along the street, suggesting that they were planned and built at the same time.

This impression of planning is reinforced by a study of the buildings. About 90 units have now been identified, of which 65 have been excavated to at least the latest floors. All are built of roughly-finished local stone, and the majority of them conform to a single plan, with minor variations. In its simplest form this plan consists of two rooms, an outer L-shaped area and a smaller, inner room. The inner room was normally roofed, but it is not entirely clear if the L-shaped one was or not. In some cases it may have been, but in others it seems that

**3.** The stratigraphic analysis has been carried out by Robert Killick, and I am most grateful to him for supplying the following information.

there was a light *barasti* (palm-leaf) roof supported on the shallow interior buttresses, which are still a feature of traditional houses on the island today. Some of the inner rooms are subdivided, as in Building 50 for example, forming such small areas, sometimes so cluttered with tools and other artefacts that we have to ask if they were storage rather than living areas. In some cases it seems possible that there was a *barasti* construction at first floor level reached by a ladder, something which can still be seen on the island today. In others the roof may have been used as additional living space.

It is not merely the plans of these buildings which appear standardised: there is also a range of fixtures and fittings which are common to many to them. A plaster-lined basin, with a plastered stand for a jar next to it, is often found in the entrance passage. A well-furnished domestic unit had as many as three cooking installations in the outer area, each apparently for a different purpose. There are small open hearths with a clay rim, more elaborate double ones, sometimes with a clay tripod on which to balance a round bottomed pot, and well-built *tannurs* for the making of unleavened bread (Fig. 5). In addition, plastered pits of uncertain function occur, and storage jars have also been found sunk into the floors of the outer L-shaped areas (Fig. 6).

Level III represents a major rebuild of both domestic areas and the temple, but the layout of the settlement remains much the same and the buildings mostly continue to conform to the standard plan, although this is not true in all cases. The temple sees considerable modification of its fixtures and fittings, both internally and externally, but the perimeter walls are rebuilt on the stumps of the original walls (for details see Crawford et al. 1997). Level IV sees a sharp contraction of settlement, although the temple was rebuilt again and one or two new buildings appear above the ruins of older ones, close to the temple. The site was probably abandoned some time during the eighteenth century BC.

The site seems to have been depopulated over a period of time, so that only broken, lost, heavy, or valueless objects were left behind. The pottery forms the biggest category of finds, and large amounts have been found in a limited range of fairly standardised shapes and fabrics. A small amount of imported ceramics is also present, and these vessels came from the Arabian Peninsula, Iran and the Indus Valley. Other artefacts made of imported materials include simple copper artefacts such as fish-hooks and chisels, and more sophisticated status items like spear and axe-heads; stone objects include soft-stone bowls and lids, a wide range of stone pounders and grinders, grinding slabs and mortars (some of which are of local limestone), and beads, of materials ranging from bitumen to carnelian (Fig. 7). In addition to these categories of objects there are ninety-five seals, one from the temple and ninety-four from the settlement, which together with the sealings, form the subject of this book.

# 2  The study of seals and sealings

In this section a variety of approaches to the study of seals and sealings will be discussed. Each of these approaches can be shown to contribute in different ways to our understanding of the material, economic and social life of the area and period to which the glyptic under study belongs. Historically, stylistic analysis has been the classic approach to the study of seals (Amiet 1980, Collon 1987), partly because that is often all that is possible. Seals are pretty, valuable, easily transportable and highly desirable, with the result that they are often first seen by scholars in collections or sale-rooms far divorced from their chronological and geographical context. Stylistic analysis, which may include studies of materials, form, iconography, composition and tool-marks, is the only avenue open to scholars in these circumstances. It is widely accepted that style and decoration are forms of communication which can play an active role in the society to which they belong and so may be seen as valuable clues to the structure of that society (Conkey & Hastorf 1990). The information conveyed by such means is usually simple, relating to ownership, identity or status, but it can also give us information about the interests, preferences and even beliefs of that society. It is also clear that the presence of an identifiable style associated with any class of material implies the existence of certain rules or conventions in its production. Stylistic studies also suggest chronological and geographical groupings, and can point to connections with material from other periods and other areas, or to artefacts of a different sort bearing comparable decoration, thus giving the material a cultural context.

Two other approaches are particularly valuable when dealing with material from well-provenanced contexts, and are now receiving increasing prominence. It has been shown that functional analyses can yield important results, by looking at evidence for the way in which seals were used and the location in which they were used. These studies can identify individuals concerned in transactions involving sealing, and suggest insights into ancient administrative practices, and into methods for the control and distribution of goods. Such evidence can be derived from the impressions, including those on tablets and door sealings, which may offer evidence on countersigning, or of certain officials undertaking specific tasks,[4] while so-called tokens may have been used for authorising certain transactions.[5] Tags, labels, and impressions on pieces of clay used to seal containers offer other information as the backs of these clay pieces often retain the shape of the objects to which the sealings were originally applied.[6] Seal impressions are not always widely available, as it is only in recent times that techniques of excavation have improved sufficiently to allow for their routine recovery. As a result of improved retrieval, scholars have become increasingly aware of their potential.

Finally, locational studies of the distribution of stylistically related seals and sealings across time and space, both within and between settlements, add another dimension to the picture. Such studies allow us to suggest how widespread the use of seals was, the contacts of the people who used them, and how their use and their stylistic features changed through time. A classic example of this approach is Gadd's article on the Gulf seals found in the Royal Cemetery at Ur (Gadd 1932).

The following study of the glyptic material from Saar will use each of these approaches in trying to reconstruct an outline of the internal economy of Dilmun in the early second millennium BC. The emphasis will lie here partly because of the nature of the Saar material and partly because this is a little studied aspect of the history of Early Dilmun. As we noted above, much is already known of its external relations, thanks to the textual references from Mesopotamia, but this resource is not available when studying the internal economy, as no documents dealing with this aspect of life have yet been found.

**4.** See Dittman 1986, Matthews (1993) study of the impressions on the tablets from Jemdat Nasr, Ferioli et al (1994) and Zettler (1991) on the administration of the Inanna temple at Nippur.

**5.** See Crawford 1998b for references.

**6.** See, for example, the classic study of sealings from Arslan Tepe by Ferioli and Fiandra (1983).

# 3 Characteristics and current classification of Dilmun seals

The study of the glyptic of Dilmun has developed greatly since Gadd's pioneering article (Gadd 1932), and that of Buchanan, which was able to place the style in its chronological context by publishing the well-known seal impression in the Early Dilmun style found on a datable tablet of king Gungunum of Larsa (Buchanan 1965). These more recent advances are largely due to the work of Poul Kjaerum on the collection of almost five hundred seals excavated from a number of tells on the island of Failaka, which lies in Kuwait Bay, and which became part of Dilmun in the early second millennium BC. This study has enabled him to propose a six-fold division of the material, based on a wide range of stylistic considerations. Only his first five categories concern us here;[7] these are the so-called Persian Gulf seals, the Proto-Dilmun, Early Dilmun Style Ia and Ib, and Early Dilmun Style II examples. Style III is undoubtedly later than the material from Saar. In all these groups the seals are predominantly circular stamp seals, whose diameter rarely exceeds 3 cm. They are perforated for suspension and, except in the case of the Persian Gulf seals, are overwhelmingly made of soft-stone/steatite. It has not been possible to sample the stones, so detailed geological identification has not been attempted and the material is referred to generically as steatite. We will now look at the characteristics of each of Kjaerum's groups in turn.

The Persian Gulf seals are usually made from a variety of unidentified, hard, dark, often slightly speckled stones, which have not been sampled either. The group is further distinguished by a number of other features: the seals are

Fig. 9 Linear animal motif from Persian Gulf Style seal (4197:03).

small, rarely more than 2.5 cm in diameter and the perforated back has a small, high boss, sometimes decorated with one or two lines across it (Fig. 8); the height of the seal can be almost as great as the diameter of the disk;[8] designs are simple, frequently consisting of two motifs at right angles to each other; animal figures are common with occasional, schematic, human figures as well, while a foot is a popular filler motif, and the designs are usually lightly incised, perhaps because of the hardness of the stone. A drill is rarely used. A sub-group of these seals carries Indus or Indus-related signs on them, and the seals themselves tend to be a little bigger. They are also better cut, and in some cases the ratio of height to width is closer to that of the Proto-Dilmun than the Persian Gulf group.

The Proto-Dilmun group, as its name suggests, is a stylistically transitional one. The seals are now predominantly made of steatite, though the hard speckled stone still occurs, and they are larger and flatter than those of the previous group, though the diameter still does not exceed 3 cm (Fig. 10). The backs show a variety of decoration, sometimes with one engraved line, sometimes with more. The dot-and-circle decoration, which is typical of group I is always found as well. The boss is now lower and wider in relation to the diameter of the seal. The motifs become more varied and the composition more complex, while the incised lines become rather deeper. The drill is still hardly used. A distinctive feature is that

Fig. 8 Back of Persian Gulf Style seal (4197:03; diam. 1.9 cm).

**Fig. 10 Back of Proto-Dilmun Style seal from Saar (2622:05; diam. 1.9 cm).**

**Fig. 11 Back of Early Dilmun Style Ia seal from Saar 5510:15; diam. 2.2 cm).**

right angles to the perforation, and four dot-and-circle motifs, two on each side of the lines. The standardisation of the design on the reverse of the seals raises the possibility that they could have been mass-produced, though there is no evidence for this at present, and the explanation for this remarkable uniformity is unknown. It would seem to indicate the presence of formal stylistic rules.

Kjaerum has also shown that the profile of the Early Dilmun style seals varies from concave to straight, to convex, with occasional grooved or angular examples. Style Ia seals correlate strongly with concave profiles. Early Dilmun style seals often appear to be glazed with a white glaze and it is still not clear if this is a proper glaze painted on to the surface, or the result of chemical changes taking place on the surface of the stone as a result of heating. The heating of the stone is said to harden it and presumably took place after decoration (Beyer 1989, p.136).

The designs on the Style Ia seals are more complex (see below), and the figures more skilfully executed than on the Persian Gulf ones. Human figures are more common, and are shown with their torsos frontally, even when the figure is in profile; the foot is often shown with a marked heel, and the head is often schematically rendered, sometimes just by two vertical lines (Fig. 12).

animal heads are drawn, rather than made with a drill as in Styles Ia/b.

In Kjaerum's Style Ia the vast majority of the seals are circular stamp seals, and are almost always made of steatite, although rectangular examples with gable backs and a triangular cross-section are occasionally found, as are examples made of ivory, or even pottery. The proportions of these seals are very different to those of the Persian Gulf examples: the height of the seal may be only half the diameter of the obverse, so that the seals are larger and flatter, with wider, lower bosses (Fig. 11). The largest example is one from Failaka, which is 6.5 cm in diameter (Kjaerum 1983, No. 250) but the majority are between 2 and 3 cm. The boss has a standard decoration of three parallel lines running at

**Fig. 12 Stylised human figure in Early Dilmun Style Ia (5510:21).**

**7.** I would like to express my warmest thanks to PK for his generous advice, he has been the most supportive of colleagues. The basic work on classification of the Dilmun seals can be found in Kjaerum 1980 and 1983.

**8.** For a detailed analysis of the proportions of disk/base/boss see Kjaerum 1994.

**Fig. 13 Animal head with the eye drilled off-centre (L18:27:07).**

**Fig. 14 Style Ib impression (2171:02).**

On other examples, a jutting chin or beard, and pouting lips, are found. Gods are also seen for the first time, identifiable by their horned head-dresses derived from the Mesopotamian world, while bulls and a variety of gazelle-like creatures are popular figures. The deeply incised lines have an angular cross-section, perhaps made by a knife

blade, and the same tool is also apparently used horizontally, rather than on its edge, to gouge out deep, roughly triangular areas which form the torsos of human figures and the bodies of the animals. A drill is widely used, especially for the heads of the animals where a circle represents the head, while a point forms the eye. The nose, ears, and horns, if appropriate, are then added afterwards.

A detailed examination of the tool-marks on the Saar seals suggests that a tubular drill was used for the heads, as circular wear marks can be seen, and the edge of the inner 'core' is slightly bevelled. The dot which forms the eye may sometimes have been inserted separately, as it is not always central (Fig.13). Alternatively, a double drill may have been used on some examples.[9] The same tool was apparently used to decorate the backs of the seals and the steatite bowls and lids typical of the period which show rows of these dot-and-circle motifs. Kjaerum (1983) suggested that a compass drill was used on the seals, but the scale is so small and the circles so regular that the operation of such a tool would be difficult.

Style Ib is similar to Ia in terms of shape, materials, tools and composition of the design, but there are also one or two distinctive stylistic features such as the clumsy attempts to show figures in profile which result in a curious hunch-backed outline (Fig. 15). Animal bodies are less bulky than in the previous style, and the line of the back is often deeply cut. It seems, on the basis of the evidence from Failaka, that the subject matter also changes slightly, with figures such as the Mesopotamian bull-man becoming more popular and the bull outnumbering the gazelle in frequency. Finally, Style II is distinguished by the use of a linear style, the incised lines being semicircular in cross-section, as if made by a burin-type tool rather than a blade, and a point drill is used. The designs are often purely geometric, and the rosette made with the point drill is extremely popular as a motif.

It can be suggested that these stylistic differences are attributable to chronological change. In order to test this assumption it is necessary to look closely at the limited stratigraphic evidence available to us. The best sequence currently available is that from Qala'at al-Bahrain, but this is very restricted in scope as no examples of Styles Ib or II seals have been found in the areas which have been published to date (Kjaerum 1994). Twenty one seals come from the area of the city wall and their stratigraphic positions can be seen on Table 1. In addition to the seals, one impression and one tag with an impression, both in Style Ia, come from City IIb levels, while a 'token', which shows the use of the point drill, and so probably belongs to Style Ib or II, comes from either City IIb or IIc.

In addition to these, there are two more seals which do not fit into any of the above categories (Kjaerum 1994,

p. 327, Figs. 1734 & 1735, Nos. 10 & 11), and which come from City IIa/b levels, and one (ibid., p. 325, Fig. 1731, No. 7), which cannot be assigned to a stratigraphic context.

It can be seen in this small sample that the earliest well-stratified seals come from City IIa and that the Persian Gulf, Indus-related, and Proto-Dilmun seals, overlap in time (Table 1). There is then, apparently, a straightforward chronological progression to Style Ia, although Kjaerum warns against such a simplistic interpretation. No examples of Style Ib or II are found at the site. If we look further afield, the collection from Failaka, thought to be rather later in date than early City II, contains no Persian Gulf or Proto-Dilmun seals; Ia and Ib seals predominate. It also contains Style II examples and the undoubtedly later Style III seals. It must, however, be remembered that many of these seals are from re-deposited fill so their chronological usefulness is very limited. The absence of Persian Gulf and Proto-Dilmun seals seems to confirm that these are the earliest in the chronological sequence and that they do overlap chronologically, as Kjaerum has already noted (1994, p. 349–50). The absence of Style Ib examples from the published City II levels suggests that they are slightly later than the Ia seals, but the area excavated is small, and their absence may simply reflect the accident of recovery.

**Fig. 15 Stylised human figure on Early Dilmun Style IB (2500:01).**

The fragmentary evidence from outside Dilmun clarifies slightly both the relative and the absolute chronology of the seal types. One Persian Gulf seal comes from Level IVb at Tepe Yahya, and is associated with late third millennium BC pottery of Umm-an-Nar type (Lamberg-Karlovsky 1973). A limited number of Persian Gulf and Early Dilmun style seals have also been found on the Arabian Peninsula. There is a Persian Gulf seal from Dhahran (Piesinger 1983, Fig. 186:11), a Persian Gulf, or perhaps more accurately, a Proto-Dilmun[10] example, unusually made of ivory, from the Umm-an-Nar grave at Tell Abraq (Potts 1998,

**9.** I am grateful to Margaret Sax of the British Museum Research Laboratory for discussions on this.

**10.** This seal shows characteristics of both the Persian Gulf and Proto-Dilmun groups, but the excavator regards it a belonging to the former group. The illustration indicates a relatively wide, flat boss, typical of Proto-Dilmun seals, but no dot-and-circle decoration is present.

| | City Ib | City Ib/IIa | City IIa | City IIb | City IIb/c | City IIc | Unstratified |
|---|---|---|---|---|---|---|---|
| **Persian Gulf** | | 1 | 5 | | | | 1 |
| **Indus-related** | | | 2 | | | | |
| **Proto-Dilmun** | | | 1 | | | | |
| **Style Ia** | | | | 4+2 impressions | | 3 | |
| **Style Ib** | | | | | 1 token | | |
| **Style II** | | | | | | | |
| **Other** | | | | 2 | | | |

**Table 1 Seal sequence from Qala'at al-Bahrain city wall.**

p. 122), an Early Dilmun style one from Mazyad (Cleuziou 1981, p. 85, Fig. 8), and five in the same style from Nadqan (Golding 1974, Fig. 5.4–8). Sadly, none of these, except the Abraq one, are in secure stratigraphic contexts. A final example of a Style Ia seal comes from an Iron Age grave at Fao, south of the Empty Quarter (Al-Sindi, personal communication).

The largest corpus of Gulf material outside the region comes from the southern Mesopotamian city of Ur, but few of the seals were in good stratigraphic contexts, and there is no useful stratigraphic evidence to be gained from this site. Once again, Style Ib and II examples are absent (Mitchell 1986). A collection of one Persian Gulf and several Style Ia and Ia-related seals has been published by Amiet. They are from Susa and all come from the period of the *sukkalmahs* in the early second millennium BC, but further chronological precision is impossible (Amiet 1972). To the south-east, a few Early Dilmun style seals are known from the Indus Valley, such as the well-known example from Lothal, but accurate dating is not possible here either (Rao 1986).

Absolute dates for the use of these seals are again mainly provided by the sequence at Qala'at al-Bahrain. The two seals associated with Umm-an-Nar pottery at Yahya and at Abraq strengthen the case for suggesting that the Persian Gulf seals do pre-date the Early Dilmun style ones, and that they are first found in late third millennium BC levels, although they would appear to continue in use alongside the later styles. At Qala'at al-Bahrain, as we have seen, seals are first found in the earliest level of City II, a level to which Højlund has given an absolute date of between 2200 and 2100 BC. Style Ia began a little later, in City IIb, perhaps around 2000 BC. The famous impression of a Style Ia seal on a tablet of Gungunum of Larsa would fit neatly into this scheme as this king is generally thought to have reigned around 1920 BC (Buchanan 1965). Seals are found until the end of City IIc and this suggests a minimum span for the existence of the Persian Gulf and Early Dilmun style seals of around 300 and a maximum of 400 years, in absolute terms from about 2200–1800 BC.

In a recent work, Gasche puts forward a case based on archaeological, textual and astronomical evidence for adopting the so-called 'Low Chronology' for Hammurabi of Babylon, thus lowering all the dates for second millennium BC Mesopotamian history by around 100 years (Gasche et al. 1998). This scheme would put the fall of Ur and the beginning of the Isin–Larsa period about 1911 BC, and the death of Gungunum as late as 1811 BC. The period when the trade between Mesopotamia and Dilmun was at its height would then date from around 1910–1700 BC, ending during the reign of Hammurabi.

This lowering of the dates for Hammurabi would create real problems for the chronology of the Gulf and does not match the chronology proposed by Højlund nor the radio-carbon determinations from Saar, which suggest that the settlement came to an end during the nineteenth century, at a time prior to the end of City IIc (Crawford et al. 1997, Fig. 126). The end of the Saar settlement cannot be precisely dated, nor exactly correlated with the sequence at Qala'at al-Bahrain, but probably belongs to a period between 1900–1800 BC. The single C14 determination from the Barbar temple, also approximately contemporary, suggests a similar chronological framework. If the proposed new dates for Hammurabi are accepted, this is a time when the Dilmun trade was at its height, and we might expect to see expansion rather than decline on the islands. These problems are not touched on by Gasche and his colleagues. The Gulf evidence presently available favours the so-called 'Middle Chronology' for Hammurabi rather than the low one.

The limited stratigraphic evidence available to us makes it difficult to state with confidence that the stylistic changes noted by Kjaerum are due solely to differences in date, and suggests that we should begin to consider other possible explanations as well. The idea that some of the observed stylistic differences reflect regional groupings, or the output of different workshops, rather than chronological change, is not new, but needs to be explored further (Kjaerum 1994, p. 341). The archaeological evidence is again still too meagre to allow us to come to a conclusion. There is currently some archaeological evidence for two workshops within Dilmun, one on Failaka (Ciarli 1990, pp. 467–491) and the other at Qala'at al-Bahrain, though the seal blanks from this site come from a variety of different levels and locations and may be the product of more than one production centre (Kjaerum 1994, pp. 337–340). In neither case could a specific style be associated with the proposed workshop. At each site Style Ia seals predominate, which might suggest that this group of seals was produced at both sites. On the other hand, we can also speculate that the very distinctive sub-group of Persian Gulf seals with Indus Valley signs on them may well represent the product of a specialised workshop whose location is unknown.

# 4 Stylistic analysis of seals and sealings from Saar

This section will use the three approaches discussed above, stylistic, functional and locational, to study the relatively large and varied corpus of well-stratified, well-dated glyptic material from Saar. The aims of the study are: to continue the task of reconstructing the social and economic life of a large village or small town of the early second millennium BC on the main island of Bahrain; to look at the external contacts suggested by the designs on the glyptic; and to explore whether any modifications of the existing stylistic and chronological classification can be suggested.

A total of ninety-five seals and fragments of seals have been recovered from Saar, all of them of Persian Gulf, Proto-Dilmun, or Early Dilmun Style I types. Five or six can be attributed to the Persian Gulf group and three to the Proto-Dilmun, one to Early Dilmun Ib, and another to either Early Dilmun group Ib or group II; the rest all belong to group Ia. It is more difficult to be precise about the number of sealings found, as many are extremely friable and very fragmentary. More than two hundred and twenty sealings or fragments of sealings have been registered, and many entries consist of a number of small pieces. Most of the sealings are made of good quality fine clay, which takes a clear impression, although inclusions are sometimes present, and many show clear finger-prints round the sides of the impression, where it was pressed onto the container. All the designs are in one of the local styles: there are none from outside Dilmun. It is probably accurate to say that about a fifth of the total have no visible design on them, while many of the remainder have only individual or damaged motifs. About ten percent are well enough preserved to be able to reconstruct the whole composition, and all but one of these are in the Early Dilmun Style I tradition, the great majority belonging to Style Ia. Rather surprisingly, no instance has been

found of an impression which was made with a seal found at Saar, though there are many close parallels in the designs. There are no sealings from Persian Gulf seals, and only one which appears to be from a Proto-Dilmun seal (1105:02[12]). A very small number of Style Ib impressions have been identified (for example, 2171:02, 5176:07).

A final group of sealed material is provided by fourteen tokens, most of which have already been published (Crawford 1998b), and nine tags, labels and bullae, all of which are also impressed with Early Dilmun style designs.

These seals and sealings represent the best-documented and most varied collection of glyptic material from the Gulf region in the early second millennium BC.[13] Although perhaps four times as many seals have been found at Failaka, there are hardly any seal impressions from this site and many of the finds are poorly stratified, as we saw above. The corpus from Qala'at al-Bahrain is much smaller than that from Saar, comprising twenty-one complete seals, one seal impression on a jar, one tag, one token and a number of seal blanks (see above p. 18, & Kjaerum 1994).

The Saar seals are closely similar to previously published examples, in shape, size and materials. Amongst the Persian Gulf seals the stone appears to the naked eye to be rather harder than the soft steatite used for the Early Dilmun style seals, which may help explain the simplicity of the designs and shallowness of the cutting on this group. Amongst the Early Dilmun style examples almost all are of steatite. Exceptions are: one example made of reddish clay (5196:01), one, or possibly two, of ivory (1098:03, 2109:01) and one made of a curious, mottled, red stone, white on the surface (5155:10). There is also a small group of four shell disks, made from the apex of conch shells, which may be seals. Two are perforated (2142:11, Q20:22:07), but the

**12.** This represents the Saar catalogue number. The digits before the colon are the context number, those after, the object number.

**13.** For the chronology see opposite.

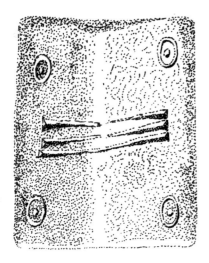

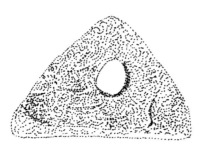

**Fig. 16 Rectilinear seal (I14:20:10; 1.2 x 1.5 cm).**

there is one with a button back (6581:02), one undecorated example (2622:05), and one with a single line (4197:03). The Proto-Dilmun examples carry the dot-and-circle motifs typical of the Early Dilmun style seals, but the number of lines across the boss varies. The Early Dilmun style seals are also close to previously published ones: all but five of them are round, perforated stamp seals, with a standardised decoration on the reverse of three lines and four dot-and-circle motifs. Even the four rectilinear seals (1098:03, 5196:01, 6535:01, & I14:20:10), of which one is ivory and one ceramic, have the same design on the backs (Fig. 16). Most of the seals show traces of glaze (Beyer 1989). A single cylinder seal (4741:11), made of creamy white stone, completes the collection from Saar. In spite of its shape, the style of the cylinder seal is unmistakably Early Dilmun, and closely comparable examples have been found at Ur, Susa and on Failaka (Al Gailani-Werr 1986).

The accepted classification of Early Dilmun period seals used form, design motifs and principles of composition which can be one of the most useful diagnostic criteria in classifying glyptic art (Matthews 1990). If we look at the Saar corpus, marked differences in composition are seen between the Persian Gulf and Early Dilmun style examples. The Persian Gulf seals appear to be designed according to different formal principles from the Early Dilmun ones. They typically show one or two figures, usually of animals, often arranged one above the other, with one figure inverted and at right angles to the first. Where inscriptions in the Indus script are found, they normally lie round the periphery of one segment of the seal. Filler motifs may be scattered across the surface of the seal in an apparently random manner. With the Proto-Dilmun seals the motifs begin to be better disciplined, and integrated scenes are depicted.

The composition of the Early Dilmun style designs is much more complex, and varies from the very formal to the chaotic. The formal designs frequently show two opposing figures, often a human and an animal, on opposite sides of a central motif such as a branch or a tree (4350:01 or 6583:01), and the feet of the figures are carefully aligned at the same level. By contrast, the chaotic designs have human and animal figures leaping across the surface of the seal at a variety of heights (see 2570:01).

Other compositions include a particularly interesting group of seals which shows rotating designs, often composed of animal heads, with the necks joined in the centre of the seal to form a sort of wheel (Fig. 17). These are much less common than the types discussed above: only two seals with this design were found (G17:18:02 &

others (5039:01, 7003:29) may not have been seals at all, as they are unperforated, and could have been counters or gamesmen of some sort. None of the Saar shell seals have the simple engraved figures or patterns found on the obverse of shell seals from other sites (Al-Khalifa 1986). These engraved shell disks have the strongest claim to be considered as genuine seals.

The Persian Gulf seals in the Saar corpus are similar in shape and size to those previously published, and the backs show a variety of decorations.[14] For example,

Fig. 17 Rotating animal heads
(7008:05; diam. 2.64 cm).

7008:05). A closely related impression showing four animal heads can be seen on one side of a tag (2070:11). Similar rotating designs are found at the Barbar temple, and on Failaka (Beyer 1989, Nos. 278–280; Kjaerum 1983, Nos. 1 & 3). This design was first discussed by Porada in a seminal article (Porada 1974), and since then it has been possible to extend the parallels which she noted from Syro–Anatolia to include more examples from the Indus Valley and Central Asia, most of which also date to the first quarter of the second millennium BC.

Other compositions identified on the Saar seals include files of figures (K16:29:03), well-known from Failaka, seals where the surface is divided into four quarters with a different motif in each (as on 2535:01), and one example of a mirror-image design, where the same figures are repeated first in one plane

and then at 180° (1024:06). A broken impression from the temple apparently shows a similar type of design (1612:10; Crawford and Matthews 1997, p. 109), and it too occurs occasionally on Failaka (Kjaerum 1983, No. 217). On rare examples two registers, or perhaps more accurately two superimposed designs, are seen, as on 4025:14.

The two most favoured compositions on the Early Dilmun style seals are the opposed figures described above, which form about 18% of the designs, and a design dominated by a single figure with subsidiary motifs around it (Fig. 18), which is found on about 20% of examples. These two compositions account for 48% of the total. Only about thirty of the seal impressions are complete enough to establish the composition of the design, and here opposed designs account for 30% of the whole, and designs dominated by a single figure for roughly 15%, giving 45% of the total available for study, a comparable figure to that noted for the seals.

The subject matter of the Persian Gulf seals is also very different from that of the Early Dilmun style examples. As we saw above, the Persian Gulf seals often depict one or more animals in a rather random association. Unusually, one seal from Saar (4139:01) shows a schematic human figure of indeterminate sex with arms and legs wide apart, but human figures are rare and crudely portrayed. A foot is a popular filler motif, and insects and birds are also found. (For a full discussion see Kjaerum 1994, table on p. 342 and accompanying text.) Similar scenes remain popular on Proto-Dilmun examples, and simple scenes of people drinking or sailing in a boat are also found.

By contrast, the scenes portrayed on the Early Dilmun style Saar seals are extremely varied, and almost all are figurative, with animals in particular depicted with great vitality. Many scenes show an elegant horned

**Fig. 18 Single human figure with subsidiary motifs (1870:18; diam. 2.46 cm).**

**14.** See for example.
Beyer 1989, pp.
138–140, Nos. 242–46.

**Fig. 19 Gazelle motif (1580:01).**

**Fig. 20 Erotic scene (G16:01:01).**

**Fig. 21 Hatched rectangle or net motifs (4306:07)**

animal, which may represent a gazelle (Fig. 19). Sometimes it has short straight horns, sometimes long curved ones, so it is difficult to know if we are looking at the same species at different stages of its development, or at different sexes of the same animal, or whether different animals are being shown. The gazelle is native to the Bahrain islands, and is today regarded as a symbol of good fortune in some parts of the Gulf region. The gazelle is also a favourite metaphor for grace and beauty in Arabic poetry. It is tempting to speculate that similar attitudes prevailed four thousand years ago and that this explains the animal's popularity on the seals. Bulls are also shown, but are less common than the gazelle at Saar. This is not the case on Failaka where the bull predominates (Kjaerum, personal communication). Other creatures include scorpions, snakes, turtles, fish, birds with long necks, a monkey or mongoose-like creature, and composite monsters often with horns and clawed feet.

The human figures depicted are almost invariably male, except in a small number of erotic scenes, where a female is shown with her legs wide apart, engaged in intercourse (Fig. 20). Seals showing women in a similar posture have a long tradition going back into the third millennium BC in Elam, at both Susa and Anshan (Amiet 1986). The men on the seals have schematically drawn heads, often with long, exaggerated chins, or beards. They may be dressed in long tiered skirts, in short ones, or be nude, but frequently appear to be wearing a hemispherical cap. They are shown engaged in a number of activities, and associated with a number of symbols, the interpretation of which is often difficult. Kjaerum sees the net or hatched rectangle as a podium (Fig. 21), but it may be no more than a fishing net; his 'door symbol' is perhaps a shield, with spikes at the base to enable it to be stuck upright into the ground (Fig. 22), while the hatched lozenge defies all attempts at interpretation!

The scenes involving men may show them in a file with other men, or holding a shield, or with one or more animals, probably engaged in hunting. One example shows the aftermath of the hunt, with a man striding along with the carcasses of two gazelle strung from a pole across his shoulders (Fig. 23). A seal from a grave at Al-Maqsha shows an identical scene (*Traces of Paradise*, p. 106, No. 149). On another seal (Fig. 24), a man is seen apparently riding an animal, whose ears and muzzle are slightly damaged, but which appears to be an equid, possibly a horse rather than a donkey. The first references to riding horses are found in texts of early second millennium BC date from Mesopotamia, and such scenes begin to appear occasionally on seals at about the same time (Molleson 1994). Another fine example, with a recessed border (1580:01), shows a man in a short skirt holding a horned animal on either side of him, in a classic portrayal of what has become known as the 'Master of the

**Fig. 22 Shield motif (5099:33).**

**Fig. 24 Man riding an equid (2144:01).**

Animals' (Frankfort 1954, p. 102). This is a theme with a long history in the ancient Near East and it is found in Egypt as well as Mesopotamia and Elam.

Drinking or symposium scenes showing two figures, one on either side of a jar, are not as common in the Saar corpus as they are on Failaka, but one example is present (5774:01). A unique scene (Fig. 25) shows a seated figure holding a pan balance of a type found in the Early Dilmun period graves at Madinat Hamad, and now displayed in the National Museum of Bahrain. Scales of this sort are still used by pearl merchants in the Gulf today, as well as by vendors in many less-developed parts of the world, thus providing a vivid reminder of the continuity of the strong mercantile tradition in the region. All these types of scene, except that with the balance, have parallels in the published repertoire of Early Dilmun style glyptic (see, for example, Al-Sindi 1999).

In addition to the scenes representing the activities of human beings, two seals from Saar show gods, identified as such by horned head-dresses identical to those seen on the gods of Mesopotamia, Elam and Susa. In the first (P19:01:10), a seated god drinks through a straw from a pot at his feet. He is attended by a naked human figure, a gazelle, a scorpion, and a variety of symbols. The second seems to show the murder of a seated god by a human figure who stabs him while another looks on, his hands raised in horror (Fig. 26). In the absence of texts it is not possible to identify

**Fig. 23 Figure carrying carcasses slung from a pole (1024:02).**

**Fig. 25 Seated figure with pan balance (E18:12:05).**

**Fig. 26 The murder of a god (5168:01).**

**Fig. 27 Crab motif (4306:04).**

the gods or the stories portrayed on these seals, and although it is tempting to draw on parallels which may be found in the literature of Mesopotamia, there is little justification for doing so.

Such evidence as we have from the temples of the Early Dilmun period shows no clear links with the religion of Iraq and the iconography of the horned hat may have been borrowed from Mesopotamia, Syria or Elam to illustrate a pre-existing local mythology.

It has been suggested in the past that the scenes on the Early Dilmun style seals frequently represent cultic and mythological themes, and while this is undoubtedly true in some cases, the wide distribution of seals across society and the bewildering variety of designs encourage us to look for more prosaic explanations too. Some seals may represent motifs with particular relevance to the person to whom the seal belonged, the hunter with his prey, for example, while others may be references to or visual puns on the name of the owner or his profession,[15] in much the same way as coats of arms or armorial bearings are created today to reflect the character or interests of the bearer. A seal from Urkish/Mozan, of late third millennium BC date, is inscribed with the name and profession of the royal nurse, who is shown receiving a child from the queen. Similarly, another seal from the same deposit shows the palace cook with the kitchens in full swing around him (Buccellati & Kelly-Buccellati 1995/6). These propositions would also explain the occurrence of groups of closely related designs, none of which are exactly identical. We can tentatively suggest that these belonged to members of the same family or professional group. However, it has to be said that where a number of seals are found in a single building at Saar (see below p. 41), presumably inhabited by members of the same family, no common features can be detected in the designs on them.

The motifs depicted on the Saar seals, as noted above, almost all have parallels with material from other sites of a similar date. There is one motif which, at the moment, seems to be especially popular in the Saar area. This is a crab (Fig. 27), which appears both on a seal (4306:04), and on an almost complete seal impression, composed of several fragments which come from a very similar seal (1622:04/8). It also occurs occasionally as a filler motif. A Proto-Dilmun example of a crab can be seen on a seal from a grave at Saar (Ibrahim 1982, Fig.49:6), and another example from the Saar graves, of Early Dilmun style, is illustrated by Al-Sindi (1999, p. 339, No. 262). One example is known on a seal from a grave at Janabiya (ibid., p. 296, No. 224), and another example from the Erlenmeyer collection has been identified, but has no provenience (Erlenmeyer & Erlenmeyer 1966, Abb. 18).

The great majority of the Saar seals belong to Early Dilmun Style Ia. In addition there are a few examples of Style Ib, where the line appears to have been cut with a finer, more pointed tool, and human figures are shown with their torsos in profile, giving a curiously hunch-backed effect (see, for example, seal 2500:01, impression 2171:02 and, perhaps, 5176:07). One purely geometric seal which shows the use of the point drill may even belong to Kjaerum's Style II (2109:01), as may a single impression (2141:01). These categories are not absolute, and shade gradually from one to another, so that it is not always possible to attribute a design to one group or another with any confidence. One seal (K16:53:10) illustrates this mixture of styles well, as the hunched shoulders of the central figure are close to Style Ib examples, while the high-heeled feet and the animals belong to Ia (Fig. 28). Some seals, such as K16:29:13 with its schematic dancing figures on either side of a monstrous snake, are sufficiently unusual that it is difficult to fit them into any of the existing categories.

A detailed stylistic study of the Style Ia seals from Saar suggests that two sub-groups

can be distinguished, and may represent the products of individual craftsmen or workshops as all seem to be broadly contemporary. No evidence for seal manufacture has been found at Saar itself, but as noted above, a workshop is thought to have been present at Qala'at al-Bahrain in City II as unfinished seals were found here (Kjaerum 1994, p. 337). Unfortunately, no finished examples from this workshop were identified, so we do not know what its products looked like, and so cannot link it with any of the Saar groups. The first of the Saar sub-groups is characterised by seals with a convex profile, showing spidery, schematic human figures drawn with a lightly incised line, although other tools can be used as well to depict the torso or an animal's body. Examples of this group include the man with the pan balance discussed above, a seal showing a nude male holding a shield (3302:01), and two other possible examples, 2070:05 and 2535:02. In one instance, on seal 3302:01, the main figure has ridiculously elongated legs, and the workshop may be referred to as the Spiderman workshop (Fig. 29). Similarly elongated legs, apparently incised with a burin type tool, can be seen on three impressions (1021:03, 04 and 1856:01) which may all come from the same seal. Only one example of this style is present amongst the published seals from Failaka (Kjaerum 1983, No. 65), so it is tentatively proposed that this group originates on Bahrain.

A second, 'Elegant', group consists of five seals[16] from the secular buildings and one from the temple, distinguished by exceptionally fine execution and well-balanced, usually opposed designs. The animals shown frequently have distinctive 'knobbed' or feathered horns (Fig. 30). All belong to Kjaerum's group Ia, and all include a fine 'gazelle' with its head turned back over its shoulder in a pose characteristic of the design. Five of the six have concave profiles, while one has a straight one. It is tempting to see these too as the product of a single workshop or craftsman. A similar example from Qala'at al-Bahrain (Kjaerum

**Fig. 28 Design with a mix of Early Dilmun Style Ia and Ib elements (K16:29:03).**

**15.** I am grateful to Julian Reade for this suggestion.

**16.** Nos. 1040:01, 1853:18, 2051:06, 2171:01, & 5155:10. As the last two are broken it is not possible to be certain that they do belong to this group, but each has the characteristic 'knobbed horns'. The example from the temple (1612:01) is published in Crawford et al. 1997, p. 57, Fig. 22.

Fig. 29
A figure from the
"Spiderman"
workshop
(2070:05).


Fig. 30
Gazelle with
feathered horns
(5155:10).

1994, p. 332, No. 20) is dated to City IIb/c. Other examples, from Madinat Hamad, are published by Al-Sindi (1999, pp. 123–4). The buildings in which these seals are found, with the exception of Building 207 behind the temple, all lie on the main road.[17]

A few seals from Failaka may belong to this group, but there are no exactly similar examples, again pointing to local manufacture on Bahrain (see Kjaerum 1983, Nos. 155, 157 & 161); one comparable example also comes from Susa (Amiet 1972, No. 1717). It is not easy to define further groups. For example, the presence of a recessed border, sometimes with dog-tooth decoration (Fig. 31), around the edge of a seal, which might be thought to define a third group, does not seem to do so as

the execution and style of the design inside the border vary considerably (compare, for example, Saar seals G16:01:01, 1580:01 and 4306:04).

The style of the majority of seals and sealings from Saar is typical of the Early Dilmun period but there are certain motifs from this group, and from the Persian Gulf group, which appear to be borrowed from other parts of the Near East, and which demonstrate the contacts between Bahrain and its neighbours. A study of these motifs suggests foreign links which are not apparent in other classes of material.

The stylistic links between one sub-group of Persian Gulf seals, and seals from the Indus Valley, are well known, but questions about their chronological relationship remain. This sub-group is generally better executed than the rest of the Persian Gulf group: it sometimes shows the typical Indus bull, and may be decorated with characters from the Indus script. In shape however, it fits neatly into the Persian Gulf category. Sometimes the script is used as in the Indus Valley itself, but sometimes it seems to record names or words in a language which is not the same as that used in the Indus Valley (Brunswig et al. 1983, p. 106). It has been suggested that this group was made in Dilmun, perhaps for use by merchants trading with the Indus Valley.

It is still not possible to say whether these Indus-related seals are the earliest seals found in the region, so suggesting an Indus progenitor for all Dilmun seals. The stratigraphic evidence is simply not precise enough to allow us to say whether they are earlier or later than other Persian Gulf seals. The sequence from Qala'at al-Bahrain is, as we have seen, the best stratigraphic evidence available, but here both Persian Gulf and Indus Valley related seals appear together in City IIa (Table 1, & Kjaerum 1994). Single finds of this type of seal, like that from a grave with two alcoves, of standard Early Dilmun period type, in Madinat Hamad, are also impossible to date with any greater precision (Srivastava 1991). No seals with Indus script on them were found at Saar, so no light can be thrown on this specific problem.

The question of whether all Persian Gulf seals derive from Harappan originals can still not be answered; it remains possible that Persian Gulf seals represent a pre-existing local tradition which then adapted certain foreign traits to its own requirements. One observation may point to the pre-existence of a local glyptic tradition: there is no evidence from the early part of City II for rectilinear seals, the shape typical of the Indus Valley seals. The earliest seals we have from Dilmun are circular, a shape typical of the Gulf, and only a small proportion of these circular seals carry designs which can be related to the Indus. This may suggest that a local tradition was already established before contact was made with the Indus Valley. Had square Indus Valley seals been the origin of the Persian Gulf ones, one might have expected the earliest ones to be rectilinear too. On balance, it is difficult to make a strong case for Persian Gulf seals deriving from Indus Valley ancestors, although the contacts between the two cultures are obviously of considerable importance. This is confirmed by finds at Qala'at al-Bahrain, and at other sites, of considerable amounts of pottery which apparently comes from what Højlund has called the 'Eastern tradition', and of items like the square polished weights which also originate in the Indus Valley (Højlund & Andersen 1994, p. 118).

The Early Dilmun style seals, by contrast, show little evidence for influence from the Indus Valley, probably because the Harappan civilization was already changing and waning at the beginning of the second millennium BC. Other artefacts, such as the weights on the Indus system mentioned above, continue to be found so that contact was not lost, but the glyptic suggests that contacts to the north were

of considerably more significance in terms of the iconography. The cylinder seal from Saar has already been mentioned, and this is, of course, a quintessentially Mesopotamian artefact. The fact that the design is unmistakably Dilmun suggests that a blank seal may have been brought back to the island and decorated there in the local style. Alternatively, the seal may have been cut in Mesopotamia to a Dilmun design. (See Al Gailani-Werr 1986 for seals from Ur and Susa.)

In addition, certain motifs on the stamp seals have also long been associated with Mesopotamia, most notably perhaps the gods with horned head-dresses and flounced *kaunakes* seen on two examples from Saar. These characteristics also appear on seals from the adjoining areas of North Syria and Elam, so it is difficult to know which of these was the contact zone. Other 'Mesopotamian' motifs include bull-men, popular on Style Ib seals, and some of the well-known drinking scenes. In the Early Dilmun style examples the figures often drink through a straw from a jar at their feet, rather than from a jar raised on a stand, or from a cup, as in Mesopotamia (5774:01 and P19:01:10). This scene with the jar on the floor is more common in Syria than in Mesopotamia, and the influence of this region can also be seen in the curious monkey or mongoose-like creature on a number of Early Dilmun style seals, although the creature does appear as a filler motif on certain Old Babylonian seals in the south, and on others at Susa.[18] Another motif deriving from north Syria is the bipod table with bull's hooves, which can be seen on one of the erotic seals from Saar (Fig. 32), and on others from Failaka. These parallels with north Syria were summarised by Kjaerum (1986).

These parallels in the iconography are not unexpected when one recalls the textual evidence for Dilmun merchants at Ebla, for instance, and the apparent use of the Dilmun standard of measurement here. (For a summary see Potts 1986.) It is somewhat curious, in view of the textual evidence from Ur, that there are not more unequivocal parallels to be drawn between the glyptic repertoire of south Mesopotamia and that of Dilmun. It should be remembered that the

**Fig. 31 Dog-tooth decoration around the edge of the seal (7008:05).**

**17.** Buildings 210, 207, 55, 57 and 220.

**18.** At Saar 6580:05 & impressions 1161:09, 5176:07. For an OB example see Teissier 1984, Nos. 418 & 420, and for Susa, Amiet 1972, No. 1824.

**Fig. 32
Table with hooves
(4025:06).**

Mesopotamian glyptic of the early second millennium BC was somewhat formal and rather limited, but in the north the designs had more vitality and more variety, which may have made them more attractive to visiting foreigners. Perhaps we should also begin to consider the possibility that our view of the prime importance of contacts with south Mesopotamia has been skewed by the textual evidence found at Ur?

There is also textual evidence for contacts with Syria and north Mesopotamia. Six Mari texts mention contacts between Shamsi-Adad of Assyria and expeditions from Dilmun (Eidem & Højlund 1993), so it is hardly surprising that the seals too show evidence of this. Seals and sealings from Assyria itself are relatively rare and some of the best examples of the Old Assyrian style come from the Assyrian trading colony of Kültepe/Kanesh. This corpus provides a number of parallels with the iconography of Dilmun; the hemispherical hat worn by some of the male figures on Early Dilmun style seals can be seen on seals such as that shown in Özgüç 1989, Pl. 91.1; the crossed animals seen on F18:33:16 (Fig. 33) can also be matched in the same group of seals from Kültepe (ibid., Pl. 82.4); the schematic snake seen on Saar seal K16:29:13 can be seen on another Kültepe seal impression (Özgüç 1968, Pl. XXVII.2); finally, the dramatic seal apparently showing the murder of a god (5168:01) watched by a second human figure whose hand is raised in front of him. This hand is depicted with only three fingers, a so-called toasting-fork hand of a type long known east of the Tigris (Teissier 1987, p. 45), and is typical of the Old Assyrian seals found across north Syria and into Anatolia in the early second millennium BC (for example, Özgüç 1989, Pl. 84.2). The other motifs discussed may originally have derived from Sumer, but this depiction of a hand seems to be specifically 'Tigridian'.

The evidence of the texts shows that some contacts with Assyria were via the important trading city of Mari, but they cannot all be assumed to have been commercial in nature. Eidem and Højlund (1993) have raised the

**Fig. 33 Pair of crossed animals (P18:33:16).**

interesting possibility that the events described in the six Mari letters relate to a single diplomatic contact rather than to a number of different commercial ones. This may be the case in this instance, but the Ebla texts certainly suggest that commercial contacts existed with Syria, if not with Assyria, and it seems unrealistic to suggest that this trade by-passed Mari. These contacts must surely have been by the well-established Euphrates route. In addition, it can now be suggested that contacts with North Mesopotamia, whether diplomatic or commercial, may also have followed a second route of great antiquity, which ran from Dilmun to Susa, and then east of the Tigris through the Hamrin valley to Assyria.

The links between Susa and Dilmun are well attested in the texts and the archaeology. It has already been mentioned that the erotic scenes showing women with their legs wide apart, found in the Early Dilmun style seal repertoire, show links with simpler scenes, with a long prehistory in Elam. One Persian Gulf seal with Indus writing, three Early Dilmun style seals, two cylinder seals decorated with Early Dilmun style motifs, and one possible Dilmun sealing from a lenticular bulla were found at Susa, and are illustrated by Amiet (1972, Nos. 1643, 1716–18, 1975, 2021 and 240). The usage of the route north from Susa at this period is suggested by a single Dilmun seal found in the treasury of the Kititum temple at Ischali in the Diyala valley (Hill et al. 1990), and by a dedication to Inzac of Dilmun by a king of Eshnunna on a stone amulet found on the island of Cythera (Potts 1990, p. 225).

There is also evidence for contact with even more distant areas. The gable-backed seals from Saar (1098:03, I14:20:10), belong to a group whose shape is typical of eastern Iran and Central Asia. These, like the cylinder seal discussed above, may also have been imported as blanks, though one of the half-worked seals from the workshop on Qala'at al-Bahrain is triangular in shape, pointing to a different conclusion (Kjaerum 1994, p. 339). It has already been mentioned that the rotating designs of animal heads found on Early Dilmun style seals can also be matched in this area, while a single example of a so-called Murghab seal, from modern Turkmenistan, has been identified in the Bahrain National Museum (Crawford & Al-Sindi 1995).

# 5 Functional analysis of seals and sealings from Saar

A large number of different but related functions have been suggested for seals and the impressions they make. All the functions relate to the central idea that the design on the seal is specific to its owner and is unique. The owner does not have to be an individual, it can be an institution, a government department or a business, so that in some cases the seal becomes a badge of office as well as an identification. The design on a seal conveys this identification to the initiated observer,[19] and that information can be interpreted in a number of different ways, depending on how the seal is being used; it can simply indicate ownership when impressed on a package, or it can show acceptance of the terms and conditions laid down in a document, much as a signature does; it can guarantee a transaction or validate it as an official stamp does today; it may even act effectively as a trademark, indicating the manufacturer of a commodity. Further possible functions are amuletic and decorative. It is possible, for example, that the Persian Gulf seals from Saar may have been used primarily as amulets, as no impressions from this type of seal have been found, suggesting that the seals were not primarily used for the practical purposes outlined above. We cannot rule out the possibility that some of the Early Dilmun style seals had an amuletic

function too, in addition to their use for more immediately practical purposes. A single seal may have played a number of different roles throughout its life, depending on the status of its owner. We may also suggest that as society became more complex the uses of the seals diversified to meet the new demands without necessarily losing their earlier functions.

## SEALS AND SEALINGS AS IDENTIFICATION

There are no clay tablets from Saar, so we have no direct evidence for the use of seals to sign or validate such documents. Clay tablets represent a technology which was apparently foreign to Dilmun, but two Early Dilmun style seal impressions are known on tablets from other places. One is the Gungunum tablet referred to above (p. 20), and the other is a tablet from Susa recording a commercial transaction involving copper (Lambert 1976), so their use for this purpose can be demonstrated from the period.

The evidence for the way the seals were used at Saar comes mainly from the marks on the backs of the impressions. A small group of impressions are bifacial, and so do not carry impressions on the reverse. This group consists of the so-called tokens (see below p. 35), and a

**Fig. 34 Tag impressed with two different seals (2570:11; 2.2 x 3.2 cm).**

relatively small group of tags or labels and disks. Two roughly oval flat tags were found, which are marked by two seals, and which were originally attached to a string, probably used to secure a package. In the better preserved example (Fig. 34) we can see a different design on either side of the 'label', two human figures and a hatched rectangle on one face, and a rotating design of four animal heads on the other. The second example (5016:02) also apparently shows two impressions, this time superimposed on the same side. It is interesting that one of them does not seem to have come from a circular stamp seal, as the edge of the impression is straight. Unfortunately the design is very damaged and cannot be attributed to a specific stylistic group, but a hatched rectangle on one seal, and a man and an animal from the seal with a straight edge, can be seen. These are the only cases where we may have evidence for what could be some form of administrative countersigning, by which goods were double-checked by two officials or departments before being sent out, with each official adding his seal in turn. This sort of procedure is discussed by Dittman (1986, p. 339), who in one instance detects four levels of bureaucracy. Alternatively, we could propose that on the Saar examples the seals belonged to equal partners in a venture, as there is no other evidence from the site for the existence of an administrative hierarchy. There are no cases where a sealing from the town has in it the sort of pinhole which was seen on a number of the sealings from the temple, and which it was suggested may have represented some checking of goods being sent to the temple (Crawford & Matthews 1997, p. 48).

In addition to these tags, we have part of another lentoid example, originally squeezed round a knot, and with a single impression (Fig. 35); there are also fragments of two circular disks with flat backs, one with string running through the centre (5210:06), and the other with string marks on the reverse (1136:07). The former has part of a design showing a seated nude figure and a gazelle; the second has no preserved design. There is also a single disk with a convex back (1029:02), apparently originally attached to a

**Fig. 35 Lentoid tag (3503:05; 3.4 x 2.8).**

string which did not run all the way through it, suggesting that the disk was suspended from the end of the string.[20] There are three more sealings which may have served a similar purpose, but they are distinguished by their shape. Each was part of a solid ovoid bulla, and all have string impressions running through them; only one (5136:06) has a fragmentary impression surviving on the exterior. In these cases we seem to have seals used for identification either of the sender or of the addressee of goods.

The Saar seal impressions seem to have been most frequently used to show provenience. They seem to have been torn off a variety of packets, parcels and jars, in the buildings where they were to be used. This suggests that they do not usually denote ownership by the person in whose house they were found for there is little point in marking your ownership of goods which you are about to use yourself. It seems more likely that the seals were usually affixed by the sender or seller of the goods and were ripped off and discarded by the consumer. Some support is found for this suggestion, as there is not a single instance where impressions from a building match the seals found in it. If this proposition is accepted then it follows that the

**19.** As the designs on all seals are culture-specific, they could presumably only be 'read' by people from a similar background. To the uninitiated, the seal could still convey the generalised idea of ownership or authority.

**20.** It is possible that this is an unusual type of token, as the design fits precisely onto the surface of the disk and the clay has been hard fired.

Fig. 36 Parallel
striations of reeds
or string on back of
seal impression
(6580:06).

designs reflect the origin of the goods and can be seen effectively as trademarks. This would explain the (rare) occurrence of identical seal impressions in different loci because we can suggest that two different households were acquiring goods from the same source.[21]

In the absence of written documents, the only evidence for the goods contained in the packets comes from the impressions on the back of the sealings, which indicates the container in which they were kept. Matthews (1993) has discussed the different impressions left by the different types of container, and has analysed the sealings from the temple in the light of this discussion (Crawford and Matthews 1997). The majority of the sealings from the settlement are non-specific, as many are extremely fragmented, and where the surface of the reverse is preserved, normally only the impression of coarse string, probably made of palm fibre, or of a knot, survives

(Fig. 36). This suggests that they came off bundles and parcels containing solids, which may have ranged from textiles and mats to foodstuffs. In a few cases (e.g. 1622:02), the impression of the angle between the neck and shoulder of a jar is preserved, suggesting that liquids like beer and perhaps oils were also items of sale. Such jars were often apparently stoppered with a plaster or gypsum bung with a piece of cloth over it, which was then tied down round the neck of the jar. Sealings were placed over the knot and on the string to ensure the contents were not tampered with. We can only guess what the contents of the jars may have been, although residue analysis might yield further information.

In eleven cases,[22] the backs of the impressions show what may be the concave or tubular marks left by a peg. The dimensions of these indentations, which averaged 5 mm where they could be measured, strongly suggests that we are looking at small pegs of a sort used to close boxes, rather than at door pegs. A study of the peg impressions from the Ash Pit at Abu Salabikh in Iraq found that door pegs averaged 28 mm in diameter, while those thought to have been used on boxes had a diameter of 8.9 mm, with one of only 3.5 mm (Crawford & Matthews 1997, p. 51; Martin & Matthews 1993, p. 38). Three of these impressions are found close together in Building 220 at Saar,[23] where one actually lies in a doorway, and two of them bear the same design, but apart from these three, the examples are found scattered across the buildings. If these were the impressions left by breaking the seals on doors, then we would expect to find several of them in the same context, representing a number of different openings of the door. It would seem strange to seal a door only once in the life of a building. (Perhaps it could be argued that there may have been less need to secure stores or strong rooms in private houses than in public buildings.)

Theoretically it should be possible to estimate the quantities of sealed goods entering the different buildings in the settlement, and so obtain some indication of their relative prosperity by counting the numbers of seal impressions found, but it is difficult to estimate the quantity of goods involved, because there is clear evidence in at least one instance of multiple sealings being applied to a single container. A cooking pot (1042:14) was surrounded by five sealings, all decorated with parts of the same design of two horned animals rampant, on either side of a turtle. The sealings

Fig. 37 Seven separate impressions of the same seal are combined here to show the overall design (1853:97 et al.).

Fig. 38 Token (2126:01; diam. 1.5).

had apparently fallen from the pot. (This is another instance where it seems reasonable to suggest that the seal acted as a trademark.) In a second example, eleven fragments with multiple impressions from the same seal were found close together in one area of Building 207, suggesting that they too may have come from a single consignment of goods.[24]

Information on the contents of this considerable variety of containers, as we have seen, is virtually non-existent, but the fact that the seal impressions are all in the local Dilmun tradition, strongly suggests that the goods, whatever they were, were packed and dispatched from within the Dilmun polity, and in many case from the immediate vicinity of Saar. This conclusion is supported by a small programme of analyses kindly undertaken by Dr Gerwulf Schneider at the Freie Universität, Berlin. Six sealings were analysed to establish their chemical composition and were shown to have originated from three different sources, none of which matched the clay sources used for the pottery (Table 2). All these sources appear to lie in the neighbourhood of Saar and the clays certainly did not originate outside Bahrain. The six samples processed represent about 2% of the total corpus of sealings, so that it would seem statistically probable that a larger sample would identify a number of other sources of clay. These analyses certainly support the proposal that there was a lively

local trade around the settlement at Saar. Dilmun in the early second millennium BC also included the Eastern Province of Arabia and the island of Failaka, so that there was ample opportunity for further trade with these areas as well.

It is also possible that some of the imported goods found at Saar, like the carnelian beads or the copper, may have been repacked at the point of entry, and forwarded on by the importer. However, materials such as the bitumen found at the site, which was of Iranian origin, was probably imported direct, as we know that the bitumen from Qala'at al-Bahrain, the most likely redistribution centre, originated from the Middle Euphrates (Connan et al. 1998).

## SEALS AS AUTHORISATION?

A group of fourteen artefacts form a specific sub-group within the Saar glyptic material, and have been called tokens. Eight of them have already been published (Crawford 1998b), and a further six can now be added. All are small, circular or sub-circular pieces of fine clay, carefully formed into bifacial pellets (four examples), or button-shaped objects with hemispherical backs (ten examples); three of the fourteen are incomplete and therefore their identification as tokens could be questioned (1159:05 & 07, 5176:02). Three of the button-shaped examples are pierced for

**21.** For instance 1853:95, which has a design of a seated man facing a type of *caduceus*, is found both in Building 207 and in the temple (1600:11 & 1763:09; Crawford & Matthews 1997, p. 58) while a design of a file of men (5510:18 etc.) is found in Building 224 and the temple (1596:02 & 03, ibid., p. 56). Six impressions from the same seal come from Buildings 200 and 211, one (1131:09) from Building 200, and five (1161:04, 5, 9, 14 &15) from Building 211.

**22.** 1029:05, 1042:26, 1105:02, 1161:05, 1853:100, 1853:107, 1870:06, 5147:02, 5133:01, 5153:01, 5510:31.

**23.** 5133:01, 5147:02, 5153:01. Number 5133:01 comes from the doorway.

**24.** 1853:96 etc.

| | $SiO_2$ | $TiO_2$ | $Al_2O_3$ | $Fe_2O_3$ | MnO | MgO | CaO | $Na_2O$ | $K_2O$ | $P_2O_5$ | |
|---|---|---|---|---|---|---|---|---|---|---|---|
| **Clay samples with high Ca + Mg and low Si content** | | | | | | | | | | | |
| H119 | 49.88 | 0.680 | 12.27 | 4.29 | 0.034 | 10.94 | 17.34 | 0.84 | 3.47 | 0.228 | |
| H103 | 50.21 | 0.729 | 13.91 | 5.13 | 0.035 | 10.48 | 14.41 | 1.01 | 3.85 | 0.196 | |
| H110 | 52.76 | 0.652 | 11.69 | 5.74 | 0.102 | 10.12 | 14.91 | 1.47 | 2.24 | 0.269 | |
| **Sealings** | | | | | | | | | | | |
| Hx118 | 52.40 | 0.560 | 9.73 | 5.00 | 0.042 | 9.89 | 18.03 | 1.50 | 2.54 | 0.268 | |
| Hx113 | 62.74 | 0.514 | 10.15 | 3.32 | 0.026 | 8.58 | 10.52 | 0.94 | 3.10 | 0.088 | |
| Hx116 | 66.29 | 0.575 | 10.99 | 3.88 | 0.027 | 7.05 | 6.06 | 1.08 | 3.99 | 0.027 | |
| Hx114 | 69.75 | 0.734 | 12.01 | 4.63 | 0.025 | 5.46 | 2.53 | 0.58 | 4.21 | 0.035 | |
| Hx117 | 71.07 | 0.576 | 10.21 | 3.50 | 0.022 | 6.19 | 3.85 | 0.83 | 3.66 | 0.050 | |
| Hx115 | 71.19 | 0.639 | 10.84 | 4.02 | 0.022 | 5.62 | 3.33 | 0.46 | 3.79 | 0.053 | |
| **Clay sample with high Si and low Mg + Ca content** | | | | | | | | | | | |
| H102 | 74.97 | 0.625 | 10.44 | 3.13 | 0.022 | 3.91 | 2.59 | 0.56 | 3.69 | 0.034 | |

Table 2 Chemical composition of sealing and clay samples from Saar. (Analysis by WD-XRF of ignited samples, major elements in % by weight, trace elements ppm.)

suspension, and all the decorated examples have designs on them in the Early Dilmun style; one bifacial and one button-shaped example are blank, and on one the design is too fragmentary to identify the style.

The same design occurs in two instances on two pairs of tokens. On 6539:01 and K16:53:02, both bifacial examples, mirror-image designs are found, one on each face. The design shows an arrow motif enclosed in a square, from which animal necks and heads protrude, and it is tempting to see it as a simple pictogram, especially as related motifs can be seen on a possible token from a City IIb/c level at Qala'at al-Bahrain, and on seals from Failaka (e.g. Kjaerum 1994, p. 37, & 1983, Nos. 52–3). Another

arrow-shaped motif can be seen on the blade of a chisel or axe in the collection of the National Museum of Bahrain (Lombard & Kervran 1989, p. 169, No. 314). The second pair, this time of unifacial tokens, both show a geometric design of three concentric circles with little loops on the circumference (2665:06 & 5500:27). Again, a closely comparable motif is found on Failaka (Kjaerum 1983, No. 37). Other designs are figurative, and show the horned animals and rows of standing human figures which are a familiar component of the Dilmun repertoire. One example (Fig. 38) stands out by reason of the fine finishing. It has a high domed back, and the face shows a deeply stamped design of four unusual bulls' heads, each with only one

| (S) | (Cl) | V | Cr | Ni | Zn | Rb | Sr | Zr | Ba |
|---|---|---|---|---|---|---|---|---|---|
| | | | | | | | | | |
| 3.5 | 0.4 | 121 | 168 | 62 | 90 | 75 | 2203 | 182 | 247 |
| 3.4 | 0.3 | 142 | 142 | 64 | 78 | 84 | 973 | 171 | 243 |
| 0.1 | 0.3 | 111 | 281 | 147 | 84 | 72 | 336 | 151 | 242 |
| | | | | | | | | | |
| 2.6 | | 137 | 293 | 121 | 63 | 80 | 636 | 110 | 287 |
| 1.7 | 0.6 | 76 | 158 | 59 | 45 | 82 | 502 | 352 | 786 |
| | | | 155 | 69 | | 92 | 1067 | 354 | 246 |
| | 0.2 | 83 | 131 | 78 | 53 | 114 | 79 | 633 | 221 |
| 0.3 | 0.3 | 75 | 137 | 64 | 41 | 92 | 248 | 475 | 243 |
| 0.3 | 0.1 | 87 | 135 | 71 | 49 | 100 | 280 | 487 | 216 |
| | | | | | | | | | |
| | | | | | | | | | |
| 0.8 | | 70 | 127 | 58 | 34 | 91 | 952 | 559 | 226 |

eye, and with its horns pointing towards the rim of the piece. A similar representation can be seen on an Early Dilmun style seal from Ur (Mitchell 1986, p. 282, No. 116). The back shows clearly the imprint of a thumb-print.[25]

Comparative data from Crete (Weingarten 1994), from Tell Brak in north Syria (Oates 1993), and from the Indus Valley (Franke-Vogt 1991) have led to the suggestion that these tokens were used as identification, and perhaps as authorisation, allowing the holder to collect certain goods in return for the token. It has also been suggested by Oates that they may have acted as receipts for goods disbursed, a function complementary to that of authorisation. If this is the case, then the distribution of the Saar examples is of considerable importance. The fourteen tokens are found in nine different locations, so that it is plain that we are not looking at supplies being drawn from a central store or warehouse. Three examples come from Building 220, two examples are found in each of Buildings 57, 60, 200, while one came from each of Buildings 51, 53 and 224. One was found loose in the sand above Building 224, and the final one came from Area 17, House 14, a Level II context. With the exception of this last, it is perhaps significant that they all come from buildings on the main roads in areas which belong to Level III or IV of the settlement, and where the buildings were larger and richer in imported goods than the others, suggesting a level of commercial activity.

**25.** It has been suggested that this may be a trial piece or a sample, rather than a token.

The variety of designs on the tokens also raises questions; it is of course possible that each represents a different department of a central authority, but it may alternatively suggest that individual businessmen were using this simple system to allow their associates to do business on their behalf. The token would be given to a supplier to acknowledge receipt of goods or rations, and the price could be reclaimed on its production. The presence of two blank tokens from Building 57, and one from Area 17, might perhaps suggest that someone from Saar could have been about to stamp them with his own seal so that they could then be used in this way. The design of concentric circles is of particular interest as it also found outside Saar: at Barbar, at Diraz and at Qala'at al-Bahrain (Beyer 1989, p. 154, & displayed in National Museum), suggesting that this pattern had wider recognition. Was it that of a merchant with several 'branch offices', or of an island-wide authority? It is possible that we have evidence for the use of tokens at Saar as authorisation by both individuals and a wider authority.

# 6 Distribution in time and space at Saar; ownership

STRATIGRAPHIC ANALYSIS

Saar, as we have already seen, is essentially a one-period site, which dates to a period equivalent to City IIb/c at Qala'at al-Bahrain. The earliest period, Saar Level I, which was only identified in sondages, produced no seals or impressions. The amount of material excavated was very restricted, so glyptic material may well have been present, although it was not recovered. The first glyptic material was found in Level II, where approximately 12% of the corpus of seals and sealings were found together with one of the tokens. All become common in Level III, where about 75% of all seals, seal impressions and tokens occur. Level IV provided about the same proportion of the material as Level II.

It was initially hoped that it would be possible to trace some stylistic development in the glyptic material through the life of the Saar settlement, but Style Ia designs predominate throughout, and the evidence merely confirms a chronological overlap between the different styles. In Level II seven of the twelve seals are Ia in style, two belong to the Persian Gulf group, one is a possible shell seal, and two are too fragmentary for the style to be identified. Of the thirteen seals from Level IV, nine are still in the classic Ia style, one is a shell seal, and the three remaining ones are re-cut or in some way anomalous. We saw (above p. 18) that at Qala'at al-Bahrain, Persian Gulf and Proto-Dilmun seals were found together in City IIa. At Saar we can demonstrate that they also overlap with Style Ia; they are found in Level III,[26] and in surface deposits,[27] in addition to those in Level II mentioned above. However, the numbers are very small, and some seem to have been reworked (see OOO:OO for instance). There is no evidence to suggest that Persian Gulf seals were still being produced at this

period, and their presence could be explained as that of survivals or heirlooms. In addition, it must not be forgotten that small objects like seals can be easily displaced in the archaeological record. The same could be said of the even smaller number of Proto-Dilmun seals from Saar found in Periods II and IV.[28] The only Proto-Dilmun seal impression identified (1105:02) comes from a Level IV context. The single Style Ib seal from Saar (2500:01) comes from Level III, as does 2109:01, which belongs to Style Ib or II. In addition, three or perhaps four seal impressions belong to Style Ib, and all come from Level III.[29] The overlap between Styles Ia and Ib was established by Kjaerum's work at Failaka and is confirmed by the limited evidence here.

SPATIAL DISTRIBUTION

The glyptic material is widely distributed throughout all areas and levels of the settlement, demonstrating that seals were not a prestige artefact, but were owned by large numbers of people within the settlement at Saar. Of the sixty-eight or so domestic units identified by the LBAE, thirty-six have produced seals, forty-five seals or sealings. Of these, sixteen have seals but no sealings, and seven have sealings but no seals, while the rest have both, although in very different quantities (see Table 3).

In addition, one seal (1612:01) was found in the temple, and there are forty-six catalogue entries, some of them multiple, for impressions from there too. (For a complete catalogue see Crawford et al. 1997.)

The crude numbers tell us relatively little about the differential distribution of the glyptic material, however, as the buildings listed in the table belong to different levels of the site and so are not strictly contemporary. In addition,

26. From Level II 4139:01, 4197:03, 6581:02, and from Level III 2622:05 and L18:27:07.

27. 000:00.

28. 4300:01, possibly 5147:01 from Level IV, 6580:01 from Level II.

29. Impressions 2171:02, 5176:07, M16:33:07, and perhaps 2141:01.

| Building No. | No. of seals | No. of sealings/tags | No. of tokens |
|---|---|---|---|
| 1 | 5 | 1 | |
| 3 | 1 | | |
| 4 | 2 | | |
| 5 | 2 | | |
| 6 | 1 | | |
| 7 | 4 | 1 | |
| 11 | 2 | | |
| 34 | 1 | 2 | |
| 35 | 2 | | |
| 50 | 2 | 6 | |
| 51 | 10 | | 1 |
| 53 | 3 | | 1 |
| 54 | 1 | | |
| 55 | 3 | 2 | |
| 56 | 3 | 5 | |
| 57 | 1 | 1 | 2 |
| 60 | 6 | 2 | 2 |
| 61 | 1 | | |
| 63 | 1 | 1 | 2 |
| 64 | | 2 | |
| 67 | 1 | | |
| 100 | 1 | | |
| 101 | | 2 | |
| 104 | 1 | | |
| 200 | | 3 | 2 |
| 201 (Temple) | 1 | 46 | |
| 203 | 1 | 11 | |
| 204 | | 1 | |
| 205 | 3 | 4 | |
| 206 | 1 | | |
| 207 | 3 | 31 | |
| 208 | 1 | 1 | |
| 209 | 2 | 1 | |
| 210 | 4 | 18 | |
| 211 | | 40 | |
| 220 | 6 | 49 | 3 |
| 221 | | 1 | |
| 222 | 3 | 2 | |
| 224 | 7 | 28 | 1 + 1 above |
| 300 | 1 | 3 | |
| 301 | 1 | 5 | |
| 303 | 1 | | |
| 353 | 1 | | |

Table 3
Distribution by
building of glyptic
material from Saar.

| No. of seals | Building Nos. | Approx. floor area (sq m) |
|---|---|---|
| 10 | 51 | 40 |
| 7 | 224 | 56 |
| 6 | 60, 220 | 80, 56 |
| 5 | 1 | 80 |
| 4 | 210 | |
| 3 | 7, 53, 55, 56, 205, 207, 222 | |
| 2 | 4, 5, 11, 50, 209 | |
| 1 | 3, 6, 54, 57, 61, 66, 100, 104, 203, 206, 208 | |

Table 4 Numbers of seals per building.

some buildings have only been excavated down to the top of the occupation levels, some have been dug to the primary floor, and some have been completely explored. Differences may also be due to the fact that the contents of some buildings were sieved while others were not. The ratio of all glyptic material to other classes of finds from a specific locus gives a more realistic idea of which buildings are really richer in this class of material.[30] In Buildings 1, 7 and 224, seals amount to more than 3% of the finds, while in Buildings 5, 6, 60, 63, 210 and 303, they amount to more than 2%. (For absolute numbers see Table 4.) In Buildings 207, 210, 220 and 224, seal impressions account for more than 20% of all finds, while in Building 211 this rises to an atypical 30%. Buildings 224 and 210 are the richest if both types of material are taken together. Both these buildings lie at the heart of the settlement, and we have already noted that tokens too are most common in the buildings along the main roads of the settlement, perhaps indicating that this was where the most economically active members of the community lived.

Another problem arises when considering the numbers of sealings. It cannot merely be assumed that the buildings with the highest numbers of sealings were acquiring the greatest quantities of goods, because it is also important to remember that there is good evidence for multiple sealings coming from a single item (see p. 34). For example, all eleven sealings from Building 207 come from the same seal, so might have come from only two or three packages, each sealed with several sealings; of the thirty-nine sealings from Building 211 there are five repeats of the designs on sealings 1161:04 and 1042:18, and three repeats of 1021:03, meaning that thirteen sealings may only represent three packets, while in Building 220, of the forty-seven impressions there are six repeats of the design on 5136:01, three of 511:02, two of 5133:02 and perhaps of 5176:08 as well, so these thirteen impressions may only be from four parcels. In spite of these problems it is clear that some buildings are much richer in glyptic than others: note especially Building 220 which has forty seven sealings, six seals and three tokens, and Building 224 which has twenty-seven sealings, seven seals and a token. As much seal usage seems to have been connected with economic activities, it seems fair to suggest that these buildings were more economically active than others with less glyptic. It is significant that both these buildings also contained imported material.

OWNERSHIP OF SEALS

Other questions are raised by the occurrence of up to ten seals in apparently contemporary deposits in a single building (see Table 4). The floor areas of the

**30.** Robert Killick has kindly provided this data.

buildings with large numbers of seals are not very extensive, as can be seen on Table 4, but these areas can be used for crude calculations on the number of people living in each. If we use Naroll's (1962) rather simplistic rule of thumb that each person needs a minimum of 10 sq m of living space, we have a crude estimate of between four and eight people per household at Saar. Kramer (1980) has attempted to refine this estimate by proposing that only roofed living space should be included when attempting to estimate population. Courtyards, stores and animal pens are excluded. This would make no difference to the estimates given above, as it appears that the L-shaped areas of the Saar buildings were usually roofed, even if the roof was only made of light materials such as matting or palm fronds.

These figures suggest that Building 51, which tops the list above with ten seals, all found in roughly contemporary deposits, was inhabited by four people, while Building 7 may have housed six. This in turn suggests that each building was inhabited by a nuclear family. Working on this assumption, we can ask how many members of each family owned seals. Should we assume that the one or two men in the household owned several seals each, or should we begin to consider the possibility that women and children also owned them?

There are precedents from Mesopotamia for men owning several seals in the course of their working life. In an archive from Umma, R. Mayr has identified one man who had a total of fifteen (pers. comm.), and other, less dramatic, examples are also known. A man might acquire a new seal when he was promoted, or when a new ruler came to the throne and new official seals were issued. He might also inherit a seal from his father. Women too are known to have owned and used seals.[31]

On the other hand, returning to Dilmun, a survey of the published burials shows that people were normally buried with only one seal, so there is no direct evidence for multiple ownership. Unfortunately, the funerary evidence cannot solve the question of female seal ownership either, as it proved difficult to sex many of the skeletons found in the Early Dilmun period burials on Bahrain, because the remains were often extremely fragmentary. However, there are numerous examples where the grave goods do strongly suggest that the owner of the seal was a woman (see, for example, Mughal 1983, Grave 91, where the seal was worn as a pendant). Seals have certainly been found in the graves of children. Grave 88 at Saar, a subsidiary shaft grave, contained a child's skeleton and an Early Dilmun style seal (Ibrahim 1982, p. 58). It may be relevant to note that a number of miniature seals are known from this period, and one

**Fig. 39 Building 51 in this row had the largest concentration of seals.**

fine example (5510:02) comes from Building 224, another building rich in glyptic material. It seems possible that these may have been owned by children.

If the proposition that women and children owned seals is accepted, then we have to consider whether they too were engaged in economic activities, or if the seals had other, non-economic functions. Although women may well have been both manufacturers and consumers of goods, it seems less likely that the same is true of the children. The discovery of seals in children's graves must strengthen the case for their having amuletic functions, as well as the more mundane ones discussed above.

**31.** A fine collection of impressions from the seal belonging to the Queen of Urkish have recently been published by Buccellati & Kelly-Buccellati (1995/6), and a delightful seal belonging to a midwife has recently appeared in the sale-rooms (Sotheby's 1997).

# 7 Conclusion

## STYLISTIC ANALYSIS

The people of Dilmun created a distinctive glyptic style which is first found at the end of the third millennium BC, and which survives for more than five hundred years. The presence of any identifiable style associated with a particular class of material implies the existence of certain rules or conventions in its production. The standardisation of the backs of the Dilmun seals with their three incised lines and four dot-and-circle motifs is a good example of this. Conventions are also seen in the schematic way in which both human and animal faces are portrayed on many of them. These conventions do not necessarily mean that a higher authority was dictating or imposing rules; they may simply reflect the conventions chosen by society itself. The power of such conventions can be seen in other areas of life in the Early Dilmun period too: the relatively uniform nature of the domestic architecture at Saar may be another example, and the standardised nature of the pottery corpus a third.

The glyptic material from Saar is especially important because of its range and quantity, and because of the excellent contextual information which is available. It belongs overwhelmingly to Early Dilmun Style Ia, as defined by Kjaerum, which seems to have been in use throughout the three or four hundred year life of the settlement. The limited number of Persian Gulf seals, which on the basis of the evidence from Qala'at al-Bahrain are the earliest in the sequence, continue to be used throughout the same period, and confirm the overlap seen at Qala'at al-Bahrain between this style and the Proto-Dilmun group. In addition, the Saar evidence demonstrates an overlap with Style Ia. Further, occasional examples of Style Ib seals, and impressions at the site, indicate that this style too is partly contemporary with Style Ia, something which is not apparent from the published sequence from Qala'at al-Bahrain, as no Ib seals were found here. This finding agrees with the findings from Failaka. The boundaries between these styles are not always clearly drawn, but this is hardly surprising, for, as Davis has said, 'it is fruitless to look for neat or absolute boundaries for and between styles' (1990, p. 20), especially perhaps, when chronological overlaps can be demonstrated as at Saar.

Although Persian Gulf seals are rare at Saar, there are enough of them to demonstrate that, by comparison, the Early Dilmun Style Ia seals show an increasing complexity in the designs, an increase in the number of themes depicted and a heightened technical competence. The shape and proportions of the seals also change. This mirrors the developments seen elsewhere. This study of the seals from Saar suggests that we can begin to define certain apparently contemporary sub-groups within Style Ia which may be the output of different workshops. The first of these is characterised by the linear depiction of men with absurdly long legs, engaged in a number of different pursuits and which we have called the 'Spiderman' group. The second is composed of a group of exceptionally finely-cut seals, all showing well-balanced, opposed designs, with figures on either side of a central motif. One of these figures is usually human, and the other a gazelle-type creature with back-turned head and knobbed or fringed horns. This group is referred to as the 'Elegant' group. As seals in these two styles seem to be more common on Bahrain than on Failaka, the workshops in question may have been located on the former.

The interpretation of the designs on the seals remains elusive, but the variety of scenes and motifs indicates that not all have to relate to religious or mythological scenes, as sometimes proposed in the past. Some seem to show everyday activities, such as weaving, although even in these cases the possibility that these activities were taking place in a temple context cannot be ruled out. (We can say that there is no evidence for such activities within the temple at Saar.) Another possibility raised by the present study is that certain motifs may have been particular to certain areas or settlements. The virtual absence of the crab motif from sites outside the Saar area was noted.

The closest iconographic parallels for the Saar material come from Qala'at al-Bahrain and from Failaka. Further afield, more parallels can apparently be found in North Syria and Assyria than in South Mesopotamia itself. The links with Assyria are especially interesting in view of the textual evidence from Mari, and although some contacts clearly took place via the well-travelled Euphrates route, it is also possible that contacts may have been initiated via the ancient road which ran from Susa, east of the Tigris, toward the Assyrian heartland. All these areas were linked by the presence of people with Amorite names. Such names also occur in texts referring to Dilmun, but it is not yet possible to assess the importance of people with Amorite names within Dilmun itself, or to evaluate their impact on the material culture of the islands. Contacts further afield with Anatolia and with Central Asia are also postulated. The nature of these contacts is unknown, and as the distances are so great it seems probable that they were indirect, mediated through other groups who acted as middlemen. The presence on Bahrain of small amounts of lapis lazuli, and of a few objects of undoubtedly Central Asian origin, confirms these links. Some of the contacts may have been overland through eastern Iran, others via the Indus Valley. The importance of these stylistic links must not be over-emphasised, as the style of the Early Dilmun period seals remains distinctively local, but they serve to confirm Bahrain's position at the hub of a network of routes stretching across much of Asia into the Indian subcontinent.

## FUNCTIONAL ANALYSIS

Functional analysis suggests that seals were used in a number of different ways at Saar. These included identification, 'branding' of goods, and as amulets. It is possible that the same seal was used during its lifetime in a number of different roles, as an amulet by the child owner perhaps, who as an adult could then use it for other purposes. The small group of tokens found were probably used as authorisation and identification, by both private individuals and businessmen. We cannot rule out the possibility that the design of looped concentric circles belonged to some central authority, but there is no evidence from Saar to support such a contention. The sealings provide no evidence for any kind of bureaucratic procedures in operation at Saar. There is virtually no evidence for countersigning of goods and the pinholes found on some of the sealings from the temple are not found on the sealings from the settlement. These pinholes were thought to be a simple form of checking the sealed goods. Nor are there any sealings from either the temple or the

buildings which can be firmly identified as door sealings. (At other sites such sealings can often be used to identify the person in charge of opening and closing the door.) Perhaps the private individuals at Saar did not feel the need to secure their goods in sealed rooms. The sealings also demonstrate the presence of an active local exchange system, which is otherwise archaeologically invisible, as all the goods were indigenous, and many may have been perishable.

## LOCATIONAL ANALYSIS

The stratigraphic evidence demonstrates that, as far as the Saar evidence is concerned, the different styles of seal cannot be used as chronological indicators, because no clear sequence can be demonstrated. All styles occur in all the levels where glyptic material is found.

Finally, one of the most significant conclusions comes from the spatial analysis, which shows that seals, sealings and tokens were so widely distributed across the site that it is clear that ownership of a seal was not confined to an elite. The wide distribution of this material also suggests that a high proportion of the population was involved in economic activity of some kind. The sealings seem to have come from goods in bundles and jars, which were apparently sealed within Dilmun itself, as no foreign seals or sealings were found. It is, however, possible that some of the foreign goods found at the site may have been acquired, and packaged with their own seals, by Dilmun merchants overseas, before being brought back to the island by them. Alternatively, the foreign goods may have arrived at a larger centre, such as Qala'at al-Bahrain, and been repacked there by local distributors. Even if this was the case in a few instances, the quantity of sealings found makes it likely that we have evidence at Saar for a lively trade in commodities produced within Dilmun as well. This internal trade, it was suggested above, was probably in perishable goods, like food and textiles, originating in other parts of the Dilmun polity, and is otherwise archaeologically invisible.

Although the seals and sealings are widely distributed, there appears to be a concentration of high-quality glyptic material, including the so-called 'Elegant' seals and the tokens, in the buildings along the main roads of the settlement. The majority of those buildings, that is Buildings 210, 220, 224, 60, & 51, date to Level III of the site, which dates to the period when the international trade was flourishing, and Dilmun was at its most prosperous, shortly before the accession of Hammurabi of Babylon. The concentration of these classes of material in a limited number of buildings does point to some differentiation in either the wealth or the occupations of the inhabitants of Saar, in spite of the relatively standardised nature of the architecture.

The combination of a number of different approaches to its study has provided valuable additional information on the social and economic life of the inhabitants of Saar. Perhaps the most striking finding is that seal ownership was widely spread throughout the community. It also seems probable that both men and women were engaged in small-scale economic activity. There is no evidence for the large-scale manufacture of commodities within the settlement, in spite of the presence of a single lime kiln, but this does not of course exclude the possibility that some of the inhabitants were involved in the domestic production of staples such as beer or textiles, which were then exchanged with their neighbours. The society at Saar seems to have been an egalitarian and semi-independent one, as there is no evidence for a bureaucracy or for administrative procedures in place at the site, suggesting that if there was a central authority, its rule was not an oppressive one.

Some sort of central authority on the island does, however, seem probable: Saar was not an isolated community but seems to have been part of a wider commercial system. The presence of foreign materials such as soft-stone, copper and bitumen at the site strongly suggests this, and the iconography of the seals reinforces the conclusion. Dilmun was part of a web of contacts which stretched at its furthest points from Central Asia, via the Indus Valley to Oman and the Lower Gulf on the one hand, and to Elam, South Mesopotamia, Assyria, the Syrian Jazirah and Central Anatolia on the other. The port of Ur was of major commercial significance, but we cannot at present tell how far it was the final destination for goods and merchants from Dilmun, and how far it was merely a staging post in contacts which seem to have reached as far north as the Anatolian plateau. The collapse of the copper trade through Dilmun towards the end of the Old Babylonian dynasty, partly, it seems, as a result of the devastation of Ur and the surrounding country, merely serves to underline the importance of the city.

There is still much which needs to be done. Technical questions such as the provenance of the stone, the presence or absence of a glaze on the seals, and the exact nature of the tools used, may be solved by experimentation and observation, but the outstanding questions about the origins of the seals, and the precise chronological relationship of the different styles described above, will only be satisfactorily resolved if a long stratigraphic sequence can be excavated, or if new seals are found in well-dated contexts. The question of ownership may also become clearer if, in the future, it proves possible to sex the bones found in graves with seals.

Many other questions also remain to be answered. It is hoped that in the future new evidence will enable us to clarify some of the outstanding questions about people of the Early Dilmun period. Perhaps we will be able to say with greater confidence what the internal political and social organisation of Dilmun was like, and, if we are extremely fortunate, textual evidence from the islands themselves may enable us to 'translate' some of the scenes on the seals instead of guessing at their meaning. The seals and sealings of the Early Dilmun period are a unique resource. They allow us to say with confidence that the people living in Dilmun in the early second millennium BC created a civilization which drew on elements from many cultures, and mixed them together to form a material culture and a way of life which was distinctively their own.

# 8 Bibliography

**Abbreviations**
*BTTA*: Al-Khalifa, Sh. H. A., and Rice, M. (eds.) 1986: *Bahrain through the Ages. The Archaeology*. London.
*AAE*: *Arabian Archaeology and Epigraphy*.
*PSAS*: *Proceedings of the Seminar for Arabian Studies*.
*Traces of Paradise*: Crawford, H.E.W., & Rice, M. (eds.) 2000: *Traces of Paradise, The Archaeology of Bahrain 2500BC – 300AD*. Catalogue for an exhibition at The Brunei Gallery, London.

Al Gailani-Werr, L. 1986: Gulf (Dilmun) style cylinder seals. *PSAS* 16, pp. 199–201.

Al-Khalifa, H. 1986: The Shell Seals of Bahrain. In *BTAA*, pp. 251–261.

Al-Sindi, K. 1999: *Dilmun Seals*. Ministry of Cabinet Affairs & Information, State of Bahrain.

Amiet, P. 1972: *Glyptique susienne*. Mémoires de la delegation archéologique en Iran XLIII. Paris.

Amiet, P. 1980: *La glyptique mésopotamienne archaïque*. Paris.

Amiet, P. 1986: Susa and the Dilmun culture. In *BTAA*, pp. 262–268.

Andersen, H. 1986: The Barbar temple: stratigraphy, architecture and interpretation. In *BTAA*, pp. 165–177.

Beyer, D. 1989: The Bahrain seals. In Lombard, P., & Kervran, M. (eds.): *Bahrain National Museum. Archaeological Collections. Vol. 1. A selection of pre-Islamic Antiquities from Excavations 1954–1975*, pp. 135–136. Ministry of Information, Bahrain.

Bibby G. 1972: *Looking for Dilmun*. Pelican.

Brunswig, R. H., Parpola, A., & Potts, D. T. 1983: New Indus type and related seals from the Near East. *Berliner Beiträge zum vorderen Orient, Band 2*, pp. 101–115.

Buccellati, G., and Kelly-Buccellati, M. 1995/6: The Royal Storehouse of Urkesh: the Glyptic Evidence from the Southwestern Wing. *Archiv für Orientforschung* XLII/XLIII, pp. 1–32.

Buchanan, B. 1965: A dated 'Persian Gulf' seal and its implications. In Studies in honour of Benno Landsberger on his seventy-fifth birthday April 21$^{st}$ 1965. *Anatolian Studies* 16, pp. 204–209.

Ciarli R. 1990: Fragments of stone vessels. Two case studies: Failaka & Shahr-i-Sokhta. In Taddei, M. (ed.), *South Asian Archaeology 1987*, pp. 475–491.

Cleuziou, S. 1981: Oman peninsula in the early second millennium. In Härtel, H. (ed.), *South Asian Archaeology 1979*. Berlin.

Collon, D. 1987: *First Impressions. Cylinder Seals in the Ancient Near East*. London.

Connan, J., Lombard, P., Killick, R., Højlund, F., Salles, J. -F., & Khalaf, A., 1998: The archaeological bitumens of Bahrain from the early Dilmun period (c. 2,200 BC) to the sixteenth century AD: a problem of sources and trade. *AAE* 9, pp. 141–181.

Crawford, H. 1991: Seals from the first season's excavations at Saar, Bahrain. *Cambridge Archaeological Journal* 1, pp. 255–262.

Crawford, H. 1993: London–Bahrain Archaeological Expedition: excavations at Saar 1991. *AAE* 4, pp. 1–19.

Crawford, H. 1998a: *Dilmun & its Gulf Neighbours*. Cambridge.

Crawford, H. 1998b: Tokens of esteem. In Phillips, C. S., Potts, D. T., & Searight, S. (eds.), *Arabia and its neighbours: essays on prehistorical and historical developments presented in honour of Beatrice de Cardi*, pp. 51-58. Turnhout.

Crawford, H., & Al-Sindi, K. 1995: A seal in the collections of the National Museum of Bahrain. *AAE* 6, pp. 1–4.

Crawford, H., Killick, R., & Moon, J. (eds.) 1997: *The Dilmun Temple at Saar*. London.

Crawford, H., & Matthews, R. 1997: Seals and sealings: fragments of art and administration. In Crawford et al. (eds.), *The Dilmun Temple at Saar*, pp. 47–58. London.

Davis, W. 1990: Style and history in art history. In Conkey, M., and Hastorf, C. (eds.), *The Uses of Style in Archaeology*, pp. 18–31. Cambridge.

Dittman, R. 1986: Seals, Sealings and Tablets: Thoughts on the Changing Pattern of Administrative Control from the Late-Uruk to the Proto-Elamite Period at Susa. In Finkbeiner, U., & Röllig, R. (eds.), *Ğamdat Nasr: Period or Regional Style?* pp. 332–366. Wiesbaden.

Eidem, J., & Højlund, F. 1993: Trade or diplomacy? Assyria and Dilmun in the 18th century BC. *World Archaeology* 24/3, pp. 441–448.

Erlenmeyer M-L., & Erlenmeyer, H. 1966: Über Beziehungen des Alten Orients zu den frühindischen Stadtkulturen. *Archiv für Orientforschung* 21, pp. 21–31.

Ferioli, P. et al. (eds.) 1994: *Archives before writing*. Turin.

Ferioli, P., & Fiandra, E. 1983: Clay sealings from Arslantepe VIa: administration & bureaucracy. In Frangipane, M., & Palmieri, A. (eds.), Perspectives in Eastern Anatolia. *Origini* XII, pp. 455–509.

Franke-Vogt, U. 1991: *Die Glyptik aus Mohenjo-Daro*. Mainz.

Frankfort, H. 1954: *The Birth of Civilization in the Ancient Near East*. London.

Gadd, C. J. 1932: Seals of Ancient Indian style found at Ur. *Proceedings of the British Academy* 18, pp. 3–22.

Gasche, H., Armstrong, J. A., Cole, S. W., & Gurzadyan, V. G. 1998: *Dating the Fall of Babylon: A Reappraisal of Second-Millennium Chronology*. Ghent & Chicago.

Golding, M. 1974: Evidence for pre-Seleucid occupation of Eastern Arabia. *PSAS* 4, pp. 19–32.

Harper, P., Aruz, J., and Tallon, F. (eds.) 1992: *The Royal City of Susa. Ancient Near Eastern Treasures in the Louvre*. New York.

Hill, H., Jacobsen, T., and Delougaz, P. 1990: *Old Babylonian Public Buildings in the Diyala region*. Oriental Institute Publications 98. Chicago.

Højlund, F. 2000: Qala'at al-Bahrain in the Bronze Age. In *Traces of Paradise*, pp. 59–67.

Højlund, F., and Andersen, H. 1994: *Qala'at al-Bahrain I. The Northern City Wall and the Islamic Fortress*. Jutland Archaeological Society Publications XXX. 1. Aarhus.

Ibrahim, F. 1982. *Excavations of the Arab Expedition at Sār el-Jisr, Bahrain*. Ministry of Information, Bahrain.

Killick, R., Crawford, H., Flavin, K., Ginger, H., Lupton, A., McLaughlin, C., Montague, R., Moon, J., and Woodburn M. 1991: London–Bahrain Archaeological Expedition: 1990 excavations at Saar, Bahrain. *AAE* 2, pp. 107–137.

Killick, R., Blakeney, S., Farid, S., Hicks, A., Hicks M., Kiely J., and Wasse, A. 1997: London–Bahrain Archaeological Expedition: 1994 & 1995 excavations at Saar, Bahrain. *AAE* 8, pp. 86–96.

Kjaerum, P. 1980: Seals of the 'Dilmun type' from Failaka, Kuwait. *PSAS* 10, pp. 45–54.

Kjaerum, P. 1983: *Failaka/Dilmun. The Second Millennium Settlements. Vol. 1:1 The Stamp and Cylinder Seals*. Jutland Archaeological Society Publications XVII.1. Aarhus.

Kjaerum, P. 1986: The Dilmun seals as evidence of long distance relations in the early second millennium BC. In *BTTA*, pp. 269–277.

Kjaerum, P. 1994: Stamp seals. In Højlund, F., and Andersen, H. (eds.) 1994, pp. 319–350.

Kramer, C. 1980: Estimating prehistoric populations: an ethnoarchaeological approach. In Barrelet, M. -T. (ed.), *L'archéologie de l'Iraq: Perspectives et Limites de l'Interpretation Anthropologique des Documents*, pp. 315–334. Colloques Internationaux du CNRS. Paris.

Lamberg-Karlovsky, C. 1973: Urban interactions on the Iranian plateau: excavations at Tepe Yahya 1967–1973. *Proceedings of the British Academy* LIX, pp. 280–319.

Lambert, M. 1976: Tablette de Suse avec cachet du Golfe. *Revue d'Assyriologie* LXX, pp. 71–72.

Lombard, P., and Kervran, M. (eds.) 1989: *Bahrain National Museum. Archaeological Collections. Vol. I. A selection of pre-Islamic Antiquities from Excavations 1954–1975*. Ministry of Information, Bahrain.

Martin, H., and Matthews, R. 1993: Seals and sealings. In Green, A., (ed.), *The 6G ash tip and its contents. Cultic and administrative discard from the temple?* Abu Salabikh Excavations 4. London.

Matthews, D. 1990: *Principles of composition in Near Eastern glyptic of the later second millennium BC*. Freiburg Schweiz. Orbis biblicus et orientalis series archaeologica 8. Göttingen.

Matthews, R. 1993: *Cities, seals and writing. Archaic seal impressions from Jemdet Nasr and Ur*. Berlin.

Mitchell, T. 1986: Indus and Gulf type seals from Ur. In *BTAA*, pp. 278–285.

Molleson, T., and Blondiaux, J. 1994: Riders' bones from Kish. *Cambridge Archaeological Journal* 4. 2, pp. 312–316.

Moon, J., and Killick, R. 1995: London–Bahrain Archaeological Expedition excavations at Saar: 1993 season. *AAE* 6, pp. 139–156.

Moon, J., and Killick, R. 1995: A Dilmun residence on Bahrain. In Finkbeiner, U., Dittman, R., and Hauptmann, H. (eds.), *Beiträge zur Kulturgeschichte Vorderasiens. Festschrift für Rainer Michael Boehmer*. Mainz.

Mortensen, P. 1986: The Barbar temple: its chronology and foreign relations reconsidered. In *BTAA*, pp. 178–185.

de Moulins, D. 1997: Plant material. In Crawford, H., et al. (eds.), pp. 79–81.

Mughal, M. 1983: *The Dilmun Burial Complex at Sar. The 1980–82 Excavations in Bahrain*. Ministry of Information, Bahrain.

Naroll R. 1962: Floor area and settlement population. *American Antiquity* 27, pp. 587–9.

Oates, J. 1993: An Akkadian administrative device from Tell Brak. In Frangipane, M. (ed.), *Between the rivers and over the mountains*, pp. 289–305. Rome.

Özgüc, N. 1968. *Seals and seal impressions of level Ib from karum Kanesh*. Ankara.

Özgüc, N. 1989: Bullae from Kültepe. In Emre, K., Hrouda, B., Mellink, M., and Özgüc, N. (eds.), *Anatolia and the ancient Near East: studies in honour of Tahsin Özgüc*. Ankara.

Piesinger, C. 1983: *The Legacy of Dilmun: The roots of Ancient Maritime Trade in Eastern Coastal Arabia in the 4th/3rd Millennium BC*. Unpublished Ph. D. dissertation, University of Wisconsin-Madison.

Porada, E. 1971: Some results of the third international conference on Asian archaeology in Bahrain, 1970: some remarks on seals found in the Gulf states. *Artibus Asiae* 33 pp. 331-8.

Potts, D. (ed.) 1983: *Dilmun. New Studies in the Archaeology and Early History of Bahrain*. Berliner Beiträge zum Vorderen Orient 2. Berlin.

Potts, D. 1986: Dilmun's further relations; the Syro–Anatolian evidence from the third and second millennia BC. In *BTAA*, pp. 389–398.

Potts, D. 1990: *The Arabian Gulf in Antiquity. Vol. I. From Prehistory to the Fall of the Achaemenid Empire*. Oxford.

Potts, D. 1998: *Ancient Magan: the Secrets of Tell Abraq*. London.

Rao, S. 1986: Trade and cultural contacts between Bahrain and India in the third and second millennia BC. In *BTTA*, pp. 376–382

Reade, J., and Burleigh, R. 1978: The 'Ali Cemetery: Old Excavations and Radiocarbon Dating. *Journal of Oman Studies* 4, pp. 75–83.

Srivastava, K. 1991: *Madinat Hamad Burial Mounds 1984–85*. Ministry of Information, Bahrain.

Sotheby's catalogue of the second part of the sale of the Erlenmeyer collection held in London on 12th June 1997.

Teissier, B. 1984: *Ancient Near Eastern cylinder seals from the Marcopoli collection*. Berkeley.

Teissier, B. 1987: Glyptic Evidence for a connection between Iran, Syro–Palestine and Egypt in the fourth and third millennia. *Iran XXV*, pp. 27–54.

Weingarten, J. 1994: Two sealing studies in the MBA: Karahöyuk and Phaistos. In Ferioli, P. (ed.), *Archives before writing*, pp. 261–295. Turin.

Woodburn, M., and Crawford H. 1994: London–Bahrain Archaeological Expedition: 1991–2 excavations at Saar. *AAE* 5, pp. 89–105.

Zettler, R. 1991: The administration of the temple of Inannna at Nippur under the Third dynasty of Ur: archaeological and documentary evidence. In Gibson, M., and Biggs, R. (eds.), *The organization of power: aspects of bureaucracy in the ancient* Near East. Chicago.

Unless otherwise stated all seals are of soft-stone, varying in colour from black to light grey, and have a low circular boss on the reverse, decorated with three parallel lines, usually at right angles to the perforation. In addition, four dot-and-circle motifs, two on either side of the parallel lines, are usually present.

The profiles of the seals are defined in this catalogue according to the scheme laid down by Poul Kjaerum (1983, p. 14): Variation F1: straight or convex; F2: concave; F3: angular; F4: grooved.

All measurements are in centimetres. Where a measurement or detail of description is lacking, it was not available at the time of writing.

All drawings and photographs are at 1.5:1 (150%).

Location descriptions such as 'occupation', 'floor', etc. refer to standard context types used in site recording at Saar.

## REGISTRATION No. 000:00

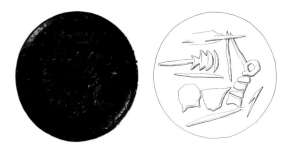

**Dimensions:** Diam. 2.28, extant height 1.75.
**Profile:** F1, convex.
**Reverse:** Traces of three, incised, parallel lines and four incised circles with central dots. Deep perforation, drilled from either end. Second attempt to drill a hole at right angles to the first has destroyed most of the boss.
**Location:** Topsoil.
**Design:** A horned animal, facing right, with its legs folded beneath it. Above its back are two filler motifs, one shaped like a churn, the other oblong.
**Remarks:** Very dark stone. Persian Gulf Style, back re-worked. No trace of glaze on either face. Drill not used. Previously published (under former number S21:0:0) Crawford 1991, p. 262.
**Museum No. 4133-3-90.**

## REGISTRATION No. 228:02

**Dimensions:** Diam. 1.7, height 0.9.
**Profile:** F2.
**Reverse:** Standard.
**Location:** Building 5, Area 20. Occupation.
**Design:** Couchant animal with a long, ruffed neck and long horns, looking up and left, over its shoulder. One horn is fringed. Above the animal's back is a hatched square (3 x 3 squares). On the left of the square is a turtle or tortoise.
**Remarks:** Glazed.
**Museum No. 3906-2-91-3.**

## REGISTRATION No. 248:22

Tiny fragment of corner of rectangular seal.
**Dimensions:** 0.8 x 0.8, c.0.25 thick.
**Profile:** Unknown.
**Reverse:** Flat, with small area of circular boss.
**Location:** Building 4, Area 33. Floor.
**Design:** Two parallel incised lines down one edge, intersecting at the corner, with two similar lines running down the other preserved edge.
**Museum No. 3913-2-91-3.**

## REGISTRATION No. 1024:02

**Dimensions:** Diam. 2.1, height 1.1.
**Profile:** F1, worn convex.
**Reverse:** Worn almost hemispherical, only two dot-and-circle motifs visible, traces of three lines.
**Location:** Building 210, Area 207. Occupation.
**Design:** A standing human figure with tiered skirt and jutting chin, facing left, carries a pole over his shoulders, from each end of which hangs the carcass(?) of a horned animal.

Both animals have their heads turned back, looking to the right. For comparable seal see *Traces of Paradise* p. 106, No. 149. Previously published Woodburn & Crawford 1994, p. 101, Fig. 17.
**Remarks:** No glaze visible.
**Museum No. 3908-2-91-3.**

## REGISTRATION No. 1024:06

**Dimensions:** Diam. 2.75, height 0.75.
**Profile:** F2.
**Reverse:** Broken off. Perforation drilled from both ends.
**Location:** Building 210, Area 207. Occupation.
**Design:** A horizontal, hatched strip down the centre, dividing the field in two. On either side are the ruffed necks, heads, and raised fore-legs of three horned animals. On one side they face outwards, to the right.
On the other the animals apparently face left, although the third is damaged (i.e. a mirror image of the first side).
**Remarks:** Traces of glaze.
**Museum No. 3893-2-91-3.**

## REGISTRATION No. 1040:01

**Dimensions:** Diam. 2.2, height 0.9.
**Profile:** F2.
**Reverse:** Standard. Brown stain on dome.
**Location:** Building 210, Area 207. Floor.
**Design:** Two horned male animals, with ruffed necks, on either side of a central palm-tree. The animal on the left looks back over its shoulder to the tree; the animal on the

right is inverted, and looks to the edge of the seal. The tree has a scorpion below its roots.
**Remarks:** Glaze well-preserved.
**Museum No. 3796-2-91-3.**

## REGISTRATION No. 1098:03

Rectangular seal, with gable back.
**Dimensions:** Length 1.91, width 1.45, max. thickness 0.9.
**Profile:** Triangular in section.
**Reverse:** Gable back, three incised lines across short axis of gable, dot-and-circle motif in each corner. Perforation on long axis.
**Location:** Building 50, Area 57. Floor.
**Design:** Hatched rectangle (4 x 3 squares) in centre of design. Flanked on each side by double-ended standard with crescent at each end. Each crescent encloses a rosette, three of which have crosses in the centre, and one a drilled hole.
**Remarks:** This seal is made of ivory. Probably hippopotamus or dugong, but not elephant. Previously published Moon et al. 1995, p. 53, Fig. 16.

## REGISTRATION No. 1580:01

**Dimensions:** Over-all diam. 2.8, diam. of carved area 2.4, height 1.2.
**Profile:** F2.
**Reverse:** Standard.
**Location:** Building 203, Area 229. Occupation.

**Design:** A central, standing, bearded figure in a short skirt, facing left, holds the horns of two long-horned male animals, one on either side of him. Each animal has his head turned back over his shoulder, and looks outwards towards the edge of the seal.

**Remarks:** The design is surrounded by a recessed area which is undecorated. The design is closely comparable to an impression on a potsherd found in the second Barbar Temple and to a seal from Karraneh (Mortensen 1970, p. 385, Al-Sindi 1999, p. 85, No. 33). Previously published Woodburn & Crawford 1994, pp. 100 and 101, Fig. 16.

**Remarks:** Traces of glaze, also well-preserved on reverse.

**Museum No. 3887-2-91-3.**

### REGISTRATION No. 1612:01

**Dimensions:** Diam. 1.9, height 1.2.
**Profile:** F2.
**Reverse:** Standard.
**Location:** Building 201 (Temple), Area 200. Floor.
**Design:** Standing, nude, male figure looking to the right. In his right hand he holds a shield, in his left the horns of a long-horned animal which looks back over its shoulder towards him. An oblong symbol in left field, and a crescent in the right field behind the head of the animal. Previously published Crawford & Matthews 1997, p. 57, Fig. 21.

### REGISTRATION No. 1841:01

**Dimensions:** Diam. 2.5, height 1.0.
**Profile:** F1, convex, worn in part.
**Reverse:** Standard.
**Location:** Building 206, Area 270. Collapse.

**Design:** A couchant, long-horned male animal, at the bottom, facing left. The neck is ruffed, the horns are straight. Above its back, centre, is a standing, naked, human figure with the head worn away. He has one arm raised to the left, possibly grasping the horns of a kneeling male quadruped. The animal apparently faces left, and though its head is worn away, it was probably turned back over its shoulder. To the right the central figure holds the hand of a second, nude, male figure, who faces left and has one leg bent as if climbing a step.

**Remarks:** Traces of glaze, also on reverse, where worn over the apex and around the edges.

### REGISTRATION No. 1853:18

**Dimensions:** Diam. 2.3, height 1.0.
**Profile:** F2.
**Reverse:** Standard. Faint scratch marks radiating from the apex of the boss.
**Location:** Building 207, Area 272, Square 25. Occupation.
**Design:** A palm-tree, just right of centre, with a seated, naked, human figure to its right, facing the tree, with one arm outstretched to touch it. Small triangle behind the figure's legs, probably indicates a stool. To the left of the palm-tree is a standing, male, horned animal, facing left, but with its head turned back towards the tree. The animal's neck is ruffed and the horns long and slightly-curved, one fringed. On the left, behind the animal's head, is a crab-like motif.
**Remarks:** Traces of glaze.

## REGISTRATION No. 1853:30

**Dimensions:** Diam. 2.1, height 1.0.
**Profile:** F2.
**Reverse:** Standard.
**Location:** Building 207, Area 272, Square 19. Occupation.
**Design:** Two standing male quadrupeds, back-to-back, with ruffed necks and horns. The long-horned animal on the right faces right, head tilted upwards. The animal on the left, with short, slightly-curved horns, is damaged, but faces left with its head turned back over its shoulder. Between the heads of the animals is a hatched rectangle (4 × 5 squares), to the right of which is a crescent. Some damage to surface in bottom left quadrant.
**Remarks:** Traces of glaze.

## REGISTRATION No. 1870:18

**Dimensions:** Diam. 2.46, height 1.01.
**Profile:** F1, straight, and worn.
**Reverse:** Standard.
**Location:** Building 207, Area 273. Floor.
**Design:** Standing man facing left, wearing short, two-tiered skirt. His arms are outstretched on either side of his waist with sharply-everted elbows. With his right hand he holds the horns of a bull(?), which stands below him and faces left. His left hand holds the horns of a second, damaged, horned animal, apparently back-to-back with the first, and facing right. In upper left field is monkey-like creature, below man's right arm is a jar. In upper right field is crescent and possible second jar. Below his left arm is another crescent.
**Remarks:** Traces of glaze, also on reverse, where worn.

## REGISTRATION No. 2051:06

**Dimensions:** Diam. 2.3, extant height 0.6.
**Profile:** F1, straight.
**Reverse:** Boss broken away, traces of decoration visible.
**Location:** Building 55, Area 80. Occupation.
**Design:** Two opposed male animals, with short horns and ruffed necks, stand either side of a palm-tree with three branches and tripartite roots. The animals face away from the tree, but their heads are turned back towards each other. Their legs are neatly bunched together in order to fit the curve of the seal. Each has a crescent above his back.
**Remarks:** Glazed.
**Museum No. 3903-2-91-3.**

## REGISTRATION No. 2070:05

**Dimensions:** Diam. 2.08, height 1.0.
**Profile:** F1, convex.
**Reverse:** Almost hemispherical. Standard decoration, worn away across top of boss.
**Location:** Building 56, Area 77. Surface.
**Design:** A male animal with a ruffed neck and horns, facing left. A figure, head damaged, cut in a linear style with bent legs, in a sitting or leaping position, appears above its back, holding in his left hand a straw coming out of a jar below. His right hand seems to be holding the horn of the animal.
**Remarks:** Possible traces of glaze.
**Museum No. 3901-2-91-3.**

## REGISTRATION No. 2088:01

**Dimensions:** Diam. 2.2, height 1.2.
**Profile:** F1, straight(?) but very worn.
**Reverse:** Standard, worn at apex.
**Location:** Building 55, Area 81. Make-up.
**Design:** Two horned animals with long, ruffed necks, one with long horns, one with short horns, stand facing each other, on either side of a fringed stalk perhaps representing a stylized palm-tree. The animals' heads are stretched up towards the top of the tree, at the base of which is a scorpion facing to the right.
**Remarks:** Traces of glaze, also on reverse.
**Museum No. 3897-2-91-3.**

## REGISTRATION No. 2109:01

**Dimensions:** Diam. 1.5, height 0.7.
**Profile:** F4, grooved.
**Reverse:** Very worn, apparently button-shaped, no trace of boss. Two dots and circles.
**Location:** Building 56, Area 93. Occupation.
**Design:** A central circle with a dot in the middle. This is encircled in turn by a rosette of lines and dots, then another circle surrounds the first. Radiating from this are four lines, each with a spike and a double volute at the end, on the outer edge of the seal. Each quadrant so defined contains a motif. One shows a hatched square attached to the central circle by a line; the others each contain a standing, horned, male animal. Two of these face outwards and right, with the head held up; the third looks back over its shoulder. The whole somewhat worn.
**Remarks:** Shiny, white stone, or perhaps ivory. For comparable designs see Kjaerum 1983, p. 18, nos. 16–17, and an example from the Ischali Kititum temple, Hill et al. 1990, Pl. 42.d. This seal appears to belong to Kjaerum's Style II.
**Museum No. 3917-2-91-3.**

## REGISTRATION No. 2142:11

Shell seal.
**Dimensions:** Diam. 3.7–4.0, 1.6 thick.
**Profile:** n/a.
**Reverse:** Apex of shell.
**Location:** Building 56, Area 68. Floor.
**Remarks:** Centre of the wide end of a conch shell (Lambis Truncata), trimmed to be roughly circular. Probably intended for the manufacture of a shell seal, but unfinished.
**Museum No. 3900-2-91-3.**

## REGISTRATION No. 2144:01

**Dimensions:** Diam. 2.2, height 0.8.
**Profile:** F1, convex.
**Reverse:** Standard, apex worn.
**Location:** Building 55, Area 81. Floor.
**Design:** A naked figure with raised arms astride an equid-like quadruped with long, ruffed neck, long ear (damaged), and short tail. Both face to the left. The animal's nose is worn away. The figure's raised right hand is adjacent to a motif which may be a star, while by the left hand is a motif consisting of a vertical line topped by an open crescent containing a circle. The lower end of the vertical line curves downwards above the animal's rump. By the figure's knee (only one leg is shown) is a possible fish, and in front of the animal a plant motif.
**Remarks:** Traces of glaze, also on reverse. Comparable designs are known from Al-Hajar on Bahrain (Al-Sindi 1999, p. 79, No. 28); and from Mesopotamia, from the site of Kish (Molleson 1994, Ashmolean Museum No. 1930.395). Kjaerum (1994, p. 346) also refers to a donkey rider on a seal from the Louvre (AO 25246). Previously published Woodburn & Crawford 1994, p. 101–2, Fig. 18.

## REGISTRATION No. 2171:01

**Dimensions:** Damaged. Estimated diam. 2.2, preserved dimensions 2.0 x 1.3 x 0.4.
**Profile:** F2.
**Reverse:** Broken away.
**Location:** Building 57, Area 74. Make-up.
**Design:** A standing male animal with ruffed neck and long horn on the right, facing right, head turned backwards towards the centre of the seal. A broken, standing figure in a short skirt, feet facing right, can be seen left of the animal. Only the feet and lower edge of skirt remain. There is a broken motif below the feet of the figure and a tree/branch motif in the right field behind the neck of the animal.
**Remarks:** Very fine and unworn carving. No glaze.
**Museum No. 3891-2-91-3.**

## REGISTRATION No. 2500:01

**Dimensions:** Diam. 1.7, height 0.7.
**Profile:** F4.
**Reverse:** Standard.
**Location:** Building 53, Area 58. Occupation.
**Design:** A standing nude figure, in profile, facing right, holding a possible standard in front of him. This is a pole with a crescent at the top and a hatched triangle, apex down, at the base. Behind the figure is another crescent, at the far right edge is a tree or palm-frond.
**Remarks:** Glazed(?). Kjaerum's Style Ib.

## REGISTRATION No. 2535:01

**Dimensions:** Diam. 1.95, height 0.9.
**Profile:** F1, slightly convex.
**Reverse:** Probably standard, but worn over boss. Perforations apparently re-drilled, obliterating one dot-and-circle motif.
**Location:** Building 51, Area 56. Floor.
**Design:** An incised cross divides the face into four quadrants. Each contains the elongated ruffed neck, head and horns of an animal. Three of the animals face outwards, with horns which are bent sharply back to fit inside the angle of the dividing cross. The fourth has short horns, and faces the centre of the seal.
**Remarks:** Traces of glaze, also on reverse.

## REGISTRATION No. 2535:02

**Dimensions:** Diam. 1.95, height 0.9.
**Profile:** F1, convex.
**Reverse:** Standard, worn. An incised line encircles the base of the dome.
**Location:** Building 51, Area 56. Floor.
**Design:** A seated nude figure on the right, facing left. One arm is folded across at his waist. With the other hand he is holding a straw which comes from a jar on a stand at his feet. On the left, a standing figure with a tiered robe faces right and holds a large object, possibly a fan, above the pot. Some damage to lower edge. Previously published Woodburn & Crawford 1994, p.102, Fig. 19.
**Remarks:** Traces of glaze, also on reverse.

## REGISTRATION No. 2535:03

**Dimensions:** Diam. 2.5, height 1.3.
**Profile:** F1, convex.
**Reverse:** Standard. In relatively good condition.
**Location:** Building 51, Area 56. Floor.
**Design:** Three male horned animals with ruffed necks. Two are standing facing each other, the third is couchant below them, facing right, looking up and back over its shoulder. Above its rump is a crescent moon.
**Remarks:** Traces of glaze, also on reverse.
**Museum No. 3890-2-91-3.**

## REGISTRATION No. 2535:05

**Dimensions:** 2.7 x 0.9 x 1.0.
**Profile:** F1, straight.
**Reverse:** Broken away leaving perforation visible.
**Location:** Building 51, Area 56. Floor.
**Design:** Central section of seal only, motifs illegible.
**Remarks:** Traces of glaze.
**Museum No. 3914-2-91-3.**

## REGISTRATION No. 2570:01

**Dimensions:** Diam. 2.7, height 1.2.
**Profile:** F2.
**Reverse:** Standard.
**Location:** Building 50, Area 57. Floor.
**Design:** A naked standing figure facing left. With either hand he grasps the neck of a monstrous creature with claws and possibly a lion's mane. Two other horned animals can be seen, one on either side of his legs looking towards him. A third stands looking left beneath his feet. Five diagonal lines below its neck.
**Remarks:** Traces of glaze, with patches on reverse.
**Museum No. 3883-2-91-3.**

## REGISTRATION No. 2622:05

**Dimensions:** Diam. 1.9, height 1.4.
**Profile:** F1, straight.
**Reverse:** No trace of decoration.
**Location:** Building 53, Area 85. Occupation.
**Design:** Two stylised horned quadrupeds, facing outwards, one inverted above the other.
**Remarks:** Persian Gulf Style. No use of drill, style purely linear. Unusual speckled dark-grey stone. No traces of glaze.

### REGISTRATION NO. 2667:03

**Dimensions:** Diam. 2.25, height 1.1.
**Profile:** F2 slightly concave.
**Reverse:** Standard.
**Location:** Building 54, Area 65. Floor.
**Design:** Nude human figure, facing left, arms raised to either side, seated on a chair with vertically-hatched seat and a high back, both uprights of which are visible. The figure faces, and perhaps touches, a hatched rectangle (5 × 4 squares) to left. To the right, behind his head, is a scorpion, the claws to the right. Below the figure is a standing animal with long, back-swept, notched horns, facing right. Four vertical lines below the neck.
**Remarks:** Remains of glaze, with traces on reverse too.

### REGISTRATION NO. 3041:01

**Dimensions:** Diam. 2.65, height (incomplete) 1.16.
**Profile:** F2.
**Reverse:** Two-thirds of boss broken away. Two complete dot-and-circle motifs survive, together with part of a third, and traces of three parallel lines.
**Location:** Building 301, Area 409. Collapse.
**Design:** Linear Style. Unusual, bow-legged, human figure, with raised arms, approximately in centre of seal. His left hand touches the ear of a bull (head badly damaged), which stands at right angles to him, facing the edge of the seal. Above its back is a bulbous motif. Below the feet of the central figure is a second, badly-damaged, horned animal facing left. Above this, and to the left of

the main figure, is a second seated human figure, with one arm outstretched to touch the elbow of the main figure. A third figure, above and at right angles to the bow-legged man, has one leg raised, and extends one arm towards him.
**Remarks:** The bow-legged figure may be compared with an even more schematic one shown on Persian Gulf seal 4139:01.

### REGISTRATION NO. 3302:01

**Dimensions:** Diam. 2.9, height 1.1.
**Profile:** F1, convex.
**Reverse:** Badly worn, especially over boss, traces of three lines on each edge and of one dot-and-circle.
**Location:** Building 303, Area 411. Occupation.
**Design:** Linear Style, stick-like human figure with long legs in centre. Outline of oval shield(?) to the left and the damaged figure of a horned male animal to the right apparently looking back at the central figure which has an arm extended towards it.
**Remarks:** Mottled grey stone, traces of glaze.

### REGISTRATION NO. 3515:09

**Dimensions:** Diam. 1.9, height 1.63.
**Profile:** F2.
**Reverse:** Standard(?). Very worn, no trace of dot-and-circle decoration, but lines present.
**Location:** Building 300, Area 401. Make-up.
**Design:** Central standing human figure in hatched skirt, facing right, and holding a straw in a jar on the floor to his

right. Beyond the jar, on the edge of the seal, is a vertical scorpion. To the left the figure holds the fore-leg of a rampant bull.

**Remarks:** Dark-grey stone, traces of glaze.

---

## REGISTRATION NO. 4001:01

**Dimensions:** Diam. 2.0, height 1.0.
**Profile:** F2.
**Reverse:** Two parallel lines only, plus four dot-and-circle motifs.
**Location:** Building 209, Area 241. Sand.
**Design:** Worn, and possibly re-cut. Seated human figure on left, facing right, one arm holding the neck of a horned animal in centre of seal. Hind-legs not visible. Pot motif between them in field. Second horned animal, poorly preserved, on right edge of seal.

---

## REGISTRATION NO. 4025:06

**Dimensions:** Diam. 2.45, height 0.95.
**Profile:** F1.
**Reverse:** Standard.
**Location:** Building 205, Area 336, Square A. Floor.
**Design:** A central, nude, female figure, looking left, with upraised arms, legs splayed and a prominent vulva. Below her is a flat-topped stand with two legs, each of which ends in a hoof. The female is flanked by two standing, nude, male figures, each of whom faces her The figure on the right touches her upraised arm and has a large erect penis.

**Remarks:** For similar stand see Kjaerum 1983, No.166. Reverse glazed.

## REGISTRATION NO. 4025:14

**Dimensions:** Diam. 2.87, height 1.34.
**Profile:** F2, worn convex in part.
**Reverse:** Standard.
**Location:** Building 205, Area 236, Square D. Floor.
**Design:** Two registers. The top register shows a kneeling, naked, male figure facing right, holding a short-horned male animal on either side of him by its ruffed neck. Both animals face him. (Animal on left damaged.) In the lower register is a second kneeling male figure also facing right, holding the tail of an animal on either side of him. These male animals face outwards and have ruffed necks and long back-swept horns, which form the division between the two registers.

**Remarks:** Traces of glaze, with worn, cream glaze on reverse.

---

## REGISTRATION NO. 4026:09

Shell seal.
**Dimensions:** Max. diam. 2.6, height 1.2.
**Profile:** n/a.
**Reverse:** Unperforated.
**Location:** Building 205, Area 235. Square U. Floor
**Design:** Design formed by transverse section cut through shell.

## REGISTRATION No. 4139:01

**Dimensions:** Diam. 1.64, height 1.14. Chip missing.
**Profile:** F1, straight.
**Reverse:** Button back(?). Perforation broken. No trace of decoration visible.
**Location:** Building 208, Area 242. Floor.
**Design:** Schematic human figure with arms raised, bent at the elbows, and legs apart with knees bent to form three sides of a rectangle, mirroring position of the arms. Plant motif between the legs, unidentified motif on either side of figure at waist level.
**Remarks:** Unusual speckled stone. No glaze. Persian Gulf Style, although human figures are not normally found on this type of seal. Simple linear style with no use of compass drill. A figure in a similar position can be seen on Style Ia seal 3041:01. Previously published Killick et al. 1997, p. 90, Fig. 4.

## REGISTRATION No. 4197:03

**Dimensions:** Diam. 1.9, height 1.5.
**Profile:** F1.
**Reverse:** Single incised line at right angles to the perforation.
**Location:** Building 209, Area 247. Floor.
**Design:** A stylised, horned quadruped, perhaps a bull, facing right, with three crescent-shaped symbols above its back.
**Remarks:** Mottled grey stone. No glaze. Persian Gulf seal. Linear style, no use of drill. Previously published Killick et al. 1997, p. 90, Fig. 5.

## REGISTRATION No. 4300:01

**Dimension:** Diam. 2.27, height 1.22.
**Profile:** F1, straight.
**Reverse:** Large perforations, small boss with three lines, no dot-and-circle motifs. Worn over boss.
**Location:** Sand above Building 7.
**Design:** Long-horned, standing, male animal with deeply incised body, facing right, and to the left a possible foot symbol. A second, smaller animal, with curved horns, lies inverted over the back of the first, its head to the centre, its body at outside edge of seal. A crescent in field between the two animals.
**Remarks:** Greenish mottled stone, reverse partly glazed. Persian Gulf Style? (Heads of animals are drawn not drilled.)

## REGISTRATION No. 4306:01

**Dimensions:** Diam. 2.35, height 0.68.
**Profile:** F1, convex, very worn.
**Reverse:** Broken, traces of three lines and one dot-and-circle survive.
**Location:** Building 7, Area 131. Collapse.
**Design:** Much damaged, and very small hole in centre, probably the result of a badly bored hole for the perforation, and of wear. Remains of a standing male animal with ruffed neck, facing right, on lower right, to right of roots of tree. Lozenge shape below and to left of fore-legs of animal. Above are one vertical and two diagonal lines, one on either side of the vertical. Probably secondary.
**Remarks:** Probably re-cut.

## REGISTRATION No. 4306:04

**Dimensions:** Diam. 2.26, preserved height 0.4.
**Profile:** F1, straight.
**Reverse:** Completely broken away.
**Location:** Building 7, Area 131. Collapse.
**Design:** Denticulated line around circumference, area within it divided into four by deeply incised cross. Two incised rectangles, one inside the other in centre. A crab in each quadrant, with thin fringe-like legs, two have three legs on each side, two have five. Each has long pincers pointing towards centre of seal.
**Remarks:** See sealings 1622:4–1622:8 from Building 203, for almost identical design. The crab is a very unusual motif, and, with the exception of one unprovenanced example (Erlenmeyer and Erlenmeyer 1966), is only known from Saar. A Proto-Dilmun example comes from a grave in a cemetery close to Saar (Ibrahim 1982, p. 158, Fig. 49:6).

## REGISTRATION No. 4306:07

**Dimensions:** Diam. 2.2, extant height 0.9.
**Profile:** F1, straight.
**Reverse:** Badly damaged, traces of three parallel lines and one dot-and-circle motif.
**Location:** Building 7, Area 131. Collapse.
**Description:** Hatched rectangle in centre (7 x 6 squares), with second, smaller one above it (4 x 10 squares). To the right a standing male figure in a tiered skirt, looking left. He touches the top right-hand corner of the large rectangle with one hand. Behind him is a jar with a straw in it. A second naked figure stands to left of hatched square, facing right, and touching the top left-

hand corner with one hand. Lower body and legs destroyed. Part of fringed motif below the rectangle, probably a crab.
**Remarks:** Glazed.

## REGISTRATION No. 4346:01

**Dimensions:** Diam. 2.5, height 1.0.
**Profile:** F1, straight.
**Reverse:** Standard.
**Location:** Building 11, Area 163. Occupation.
**Description:** Standing male figure in tiered skirt, facing right. To the left he holds a shield, beyond which is a hatched, oblong motif. To the right, his hand touches a triangular, hatched motif in bottom right field, below a long-necked, swimming bird, facing left, with a sub-circular motif above its back, perhaps a pot or a plant.
**Remarks:** Finely cut and unworn. Glaze on reverse intact.

## REGISTRATION No. 4350:01

**Dimensions:** Diam. 2.2, height 1.22.
**Profile:** F1, convex.
**Reverse:** Lines at oblique angle to perforation, spacing poor.
**Location:** Building 5, Area 25. Floor.
**Description:** Standing figure in tiered skirt, facing right. To the right he holds shield with two prongs at each end. To the right is horned male animal facing right, with long, ruffed neck, head stretched up and back, so that his nose almost touches edge of shield. Design slightly distorted to fit curve of seal. Slight damage to left side of design.
**Remarks:** Grey stone. Finely cut.

## REGISTRATION NO. 4361:01

**Dimensions:** Diam. 2.43, height 1.05.
**Profile:** F1, straight.
**Reverse:** Standard.
**Location:** Building 7, Area 45. Collapse.
**Design:** On the left is a long-horned animal looking over its shoulder to the centre of the seal, and a second, monstrous, creature, which looks outwards towards the edge of the seal. It has horns, a pointed open beak, a ruffed neck and a long tail. Its front and back legs are raised in front of its body, and the feet have large claws. Below its back legs and above its head are crescents; a four-pointed motif lies between its front and back legs. Between the two animals is a plant with a (damaged) crescent-shaped top.
**Remarks:** Reverse glazed.

## REGISTRATION NO. 4741:11

Cylinder seal.
**Dimensions:** length 3.05, Diam. (top) 1.75, (centre) 1.65, (bottom) 1.76.
**Profile:** N/A.
**Reverse:** N/A.
**Location:** Building 11, Area 163. Collapse.
**Design:** Incised border top and bottom; scene divides into two, separated by a horizontal crescent.

(i) Two men in tiered skirts, seated on either side of a jar, drinking through straws which they hold in one hand; a crescent in the field between the straws. The figure on the left holds a crescent-topped standard to the left. The crescent has a spike in the centre. (ii) Two naked dancing men, who hold another standard between them, also topped with a rather angular crescent.
**Remarks:** Creamy steatite, one vertical crack. Although cylindrical in shape the seal is in the classic Early Dilmun Ia Style and has close parallels with other cylinder seals from Susa (Amiet 1972, Nos. 1975 and 2021) and Failaka (Kjaerum 1983, No. 373).

## REGISTRATION NO. 5039:01

Shell seal.
**Dimensions:** Diam. 2.25, height 1.3.
**Profile:** n/a.
**Reverse:** Apex of shell.
**Location:** Building 222, Area 305. Occupation.
**Design:** Design formed by transverse section cut through shell.
**Remarks:** Traces of burning.

## REGISTRATION NO. 5040:01

**Dimensions:** Diam. 2.34, height 1.24.
**Profile:** F2.
**Reverse:** Standard.
**Location:** Building 222, Area 305. Collapse.
**Design:** A central palm-frond, or stylized tree, with a rampant horned animal on either side. Both animals are male, and have ruffed necks, back-swept fringed horns and flicked-up tails.
**Remarks:** Traces of glaze.

## REGISTRATION No. 5059:04

**Dimensions:** Diam. 2.21, height 0.53.
**Profile:** F1, straight.
**Reverse:** Boss broken off, perforation drilled from either end. Traces of standard decoration. Some glaze.
**Location:** Building 222, Area 305. Make-up.
**Design:** Central lozenge motif, with horned male animals with ruffed necks on either side. Both animals face outwards, and have their legs tucked under them, one being reversed. One has long horns, the other short.
**Remarks:** See almost identical example from Susa, Harper et al. 1992, p. 119, Fig. 78.

## REGISTRATION No. 5099:32

**Dimensions:** Diam. 2.5, height 1.3.
**Profile:** F1, straight.
**Reverse:** Standard.
**Location:** Building 220, Area 309. Sand above building.
**Design:** Head and front legs of two, long-horned, kneeling animals joined together back-to-back to form a single two-headed one. Both face outwards to opposite edges of the seal, and look up at two more horned animals, on either side of palm-frond. The left-hand animal is rampant, with part of one, long, notched horn visible, head damaged. The right-hand animal is a standing quadruped, head damaged, apparently looking back over its shoulder to centre of the seal.
**Remarks:** In poor condition with one serious crack.

## REGISTRATION No. 5099:33

**Dimensions:** Diam. 2.4, height 1.2.
**Profile:** F2.
**Reverse:** Standard, worn over apex.
**Location:** Building 220, Area 309. Sand above building.
**Design:** Male figure in tiered skirt, facing left and standing on a hatched platform with raised front, perhaps a boat with raised prow. One arm is raised above short-horned animal, with curly tail and claws on hind-leg, in left field. Animal faces edge of seal, with head turned back towards man. Man holds large rectangular shield in right field, with a triangular spike, possibly a spear, protruding from the centre of its lower edge. Three triangular motifs project from the top of it. A crescent lies above it, and below is a jar, between the shield and the man. In extreme right field is another composite animal with hatched body, possibly of a scorpion, and gazelle's head.
**Remarks:** Unusual red mottled stone. Glaze on reverse burnt brown.

## REGISTRATION No. 5104:07

**Dimensions:** Diam. 2.4, height 1.2.
**Profile:** F2.
**Reverse:** Standard, slightly scratched and discoloured.
**Location:** Building 220, Area 309. Sand.
**Design:** A horned male animal with ruffed neck, facing right, with a hatched square (4 x 4 squares) on its back. Possible human foot to the right of this. Rectangular motif in left field with inverted scorpion, badly worn, below it. Second scorpion in right field. There is a crescent in the curve of the tail of the right scorpion.
**Remarks:** Traces of glaze.

## REGISTRATION No. 5147:01

**Dimensions:** Diam. 2.0, height 0.88.
**Profile:** F2.
**Reverse:** One incised line only, four dot-and-circle motifs.
**Location:** Building 220, Area 310. Floor.
**Design:** Kneeling nude man with one arm raised, facing right towards long-horned, leaping animal with a ruffed neck. Below and between them is another, smaller, long-horned male animal, facing right, with its head raised. It almost appears to be suckling from the larger animal. Crescent in lower left field and another in lower right. Some Proto-Dilmun features.
**Remarks:** Patches of glaze on reverse.

## REGISTRATION No. 5155:10

**Dimensions:** Original estimated diam. 2.65, height 1.24. (Broken in half.)
**Profile:** F2.
**Reverse:** Standard.
**Location:** Building 220, Area 310. Floor.
**Design:** Top half preserved. In the centre is the head of an animal, with ruffed neck, and back-swept, knobbed horns, looking right. The base of the neck appears to protrude from the body of a second animal, at right angles, facing upwards, of which the body, head, long ruffed neck and front leg are present, and there is an unidentified motif below the leg. Human foot motif in the upper left field. To the right are the head and ruffed neck of an animal with back-swept, knobbed horns, facing left.
**Remarks:** Thick white glaze. Design finely and deeply cut. Heads are drawn not drilled. Compare with 2570:01. Unusual, red mottled stone similar to that used for 5099:33.

## REGISTRATION No. 5168:01

**Dimensions:** Diam. 2.54, height 1.1.
**Profile:** F2.
**Reverse:** Standard.
**Location:** Building 220, Area 309. Occupation.
**Design:** Seated god with horned headdress, wearing tiered skirt, facing right, his left arm raised to the right, showing three fingers on the hand. His seat has a vertically-hatched base and forked back. Facing him is a naked, standing man who apparently touches the god's waist with a stick/sword. Behind the seated figure is another standing nude male figure, facing right, with left arm raised, and three fingers of the hand visible. In the lower field a standing bull, facing right, head lowered.
**Remarks:** Traces of glaze. See seals from the Jebel Hamrin and North Syria (Teissier 1987, p. 45), and Old Assyrian style seals from Kültepe/Kanesh, for a similar depiction of the hand with only three fingers (Özgüç 1989, Pl. 82, Nos. 3 and 5). Previously published Crawford & Matthews 1997, Fig. 94.

## REGISTRATION No. 5196:01

Ceramic seal(?), broken.
**Dimensions:** 2.2 x 1.5 x 1.0.
**Reverse:** Roughly pinched into a gable shape.
**Profile:** Triangular.
**Location:** Building 220, Area 312. Tannur.
**Description:** Reddish baked clay, about half of a rectangular, gable-backed, ceramic seal. Parallel striations underneath, fibre impressions(?).

## REGISTRATION No. 5506:05

**Dimensions:** Diam. 2.3, height 1.05.
**Profile:** F1, straight.
**Reverse:** Low boss destroyed by four bore-holes at right angles to each other. Trace of line around base of boss.
**Location:** Building 224, Area 307. Collapse.
**Design:** Horned animal, perhaps a bull, with vertically-striated body, standing facing right. Second striated motif above its back at right angles to it, possibly another animal which is not finished. String of five small triangular holes in left field.
**Remarks:** Persian Gulf Style. Perhaps a re-worked and unfinished design. No glaze present; no use of compass drill.

## REGISTRATION No. 5510:01

**Dimensions:** Diam. 2.12, height 1.35.
**Profile:** F2.
**Reverse:** Standard.
**Location:** Building 224, Area 316. Floor.
**Design:** Two standing male figures in tiered skirts, facing right, and holding each other's hands, each also holding a damaged, striated, oblong object, possibly shields, towards the edge of the seal. The one on the right is full height, the other half this size.

## REGISTRATION No. 5510:02

**Dimensions:** Diam. 1.0, height 0.87.
**Profile:** F2.
**Reverse:** Standard.
**Location:** Building 224, Area 316. Floor.
**Design:** Seated monkey-like creature, facing left, holding to the left a stick or staff, with a ruffed neck and head of an animal protruding from each end. The necks curve round the edge of the seal and the heads look inwards towards a wavy line below the noses.
**Remarks:** Miniature seal. For another, slightly larger example see Beyer 1989, p. 143, No. 256. Previously published Killick et al. 1997, p. 93, Fig. 10.

## REGISTRATION No. 5510:15

**Dimensions:** Diam. 2.2, height 1.1.
**Profile:** F2.
**Reverse:** Standard.
**Location:** Building 224, Area 316. Floor.
**Design:** Well-preserved, finely-cut design, showing naked, standing, male figure in centre, facing right, and holding to the right a large hatched square with the heads of two long-horned animals, with ruffed necks, protruding towards the top and bottom rim of the seal from its inner corners. To the left, the figure holds a long shield, and beyond this is a palm-frond that lies on the extreme edge of the seal, and is partly damaged by a chip in the stone.
**Remarks:** One serious crack visible in stone.

## REGISTRATION No. 5510:17

Clay seal fragment.

**Dimensions:** Max. length 1.5, width 1.0, thickness 0.61. Estimated diam. of seal 2.2.

**Profile:** F1(?).

**Reverse:** Broken away, part of perforation preserved.

**Location:** Building 224, Area 316. Floor.

**Design:** About one quarter of obverse remains. Two parallel vertical lines, deeply incised, and another two at right angles, possibly lower legs and feet of a person.

**Remarks:** Pinkish clay with a brown core. As design is incised, not impressed, this is not a perforated token.

## REGISTRATION No. 5510:21

**Dimensions:** Diam. 2.7, extant height 0.9.

**Profile:** F2.

**Reverse:** Broken away, traces of three lines.

**Location:** Building 224, Area 316. Floor.

**Design:** Deeply incised. Two standing male figures, in tiered skirts, carrying a jar between them, and facing right. The left-hand figure holds the horns of a long-horned male animal on the left edge of the seal. The animal looks back over his shoulder towards the figure. The right-hand figure drinks through a straw from another jar to his right. A crescent lies on the edge of the seal between the heads of the men. Another is in a similar position between their feet.

**Remarks:** Thick glaze on original surface of reverse.

## REGISTRATION No. 5546:02

**Dimensions:** Diam. 2.29, height 0.65.

**Profile:** F1, convex.

**Reverse:** Standard, lines rubbed off the boss.

**Location:** Building 224, Area 316. Make-up.

**Design:** Standing male animal at lower centre, facing right, with downward-curving horns. Above his back are two more horned animals, one on either side, and facing a row of dots, probably the remains of a palm-frond.

**Remarks:** Intermediate style(?). Heads of animals are incised, not punched with drill. Traces of glaze on reverse.

## REGISTRATION No. 5774:01

**Dimensions:** Diam. 2.2, height 1.08.

**Profile:** F2.

**Reverse:** Standard but worn, lines only visible at the edges of seal, one dot-and-circle damaged.

**Location:** Area 8. Street. Occupation.

**Design:** Two seated men, facing each other, drinking through straws from a jar between their feet. Foot motif below the jar and a crescent to the left. A horizontal line joins the two men at the shoulder and above this and between their faces is another jar with two down-curving straws in it.

**Remarks:** Dark-grey steatite, traces of glaze. Design deeply cut.

# Catalogue of Seals

## REGISTRATION No. 6087:10

**Dimensions:** Diam. 1.9, height 0.85.
**Profile:** F2, concave.
**Reverse:** Standard, worn.
**Location:** Building 63, Area 306. Sand.
**Design:** Design framed by hatched, incised border. To the right is horned male animal with ruffed neck facing left towards palm-frond. On left is monkey-like creature facing right and touching frond.
**Remarks:** Pale-grey steatite, edges slightly chipped. Glazed. Execution rather crude.

## REGISTRATION No. 6535:01

Square stamp seal.
**Dimensions:** 1.56 x 1.56 x 0.6.
**Profile:** Triangular in section.
**Reverse:** Gable back. Standard decoration with lines running at right angles to the perforation.
**Location:** Building 60, Area 372. Occupation.
**Design:** A scorpion, facing left. Above is a horizontal line with a palm-frond at right angles to it at either end. In the centre is a standard topped with a crescent, with a circle with central dot (or star) above.
**Remarks:** Grey stone with crystalline inclusions. Two holes in obverse, worn through to perforation.

## REGISTRATION No. 6538:01

**Dimensions:** 2.2 x 1.2 (estimated).
**Profile:** F1(?). Obscured with bitumen.
**Reverse:** Boss broken off in antiquity, standard decoration.
**Location:** Building 60, Area 372. Make-up.
**Design:** Upper left, a scorpion, facing upwards. Below it, a turtle, facing upwards. To right, a horned male animal, standing facing right and looking back over its shoulder. By its chest, a chiselled, or possibly accidental, line. At bottom right, a bird with feathered back, facing right. In the upper right field, a crescent.
**Remarks:** Broken and mended with bitumen in antiquity, obscuring most of the perforation and the edge. Lower edge, and lower left edge, chipped off.

## REGISTRATION No. 6580:01

**Dimensions:** Diam. 1.7, height 0.8.
**Profile:** F2.
**Reverse:** Standard.
**Location:** Building 60, Area 372. Floor.
**Design:** Standing male figure with short skirt on left, one arm extended to right, touching the back of a rampant horned monster which faces right. Its fore-leg, with three claws, is raised in front of it, hind-leg tucked in, scorpion's tail. Crescent on edge of seal. Proto-Dilmun(?).
**Remarks:** Reverse glazed.

## Registration No. 6580:05

**Dimensions:** Diam. 2.4, height 1.0.
**Profile:** F1, straight.
**Reverse:** Standard.
**Location:** Building 60, Area 372. Floor.
**Design:** Nude male figure in centre facing right. To the right he touches the rump of a horned male animal with ruffed neck. The animal faces right and looks back over its shoulder. To the left, the man holds a seated, monkey-like creature, jar motif between their heads.
**Remarks:** Stone in poor condition, crackled. Animal heads drawn not drilled.

## Registration No. 6581:01

**Dimensions:** Diam. 2.4, height 0.95.
**Profile:** F2, worn.
**Reverse:** Traces of standard design.
**Location:** Building 60, Area 371. Floor.
**Design:** Striding male figure with skirt in upper centre, facing right. To the right he holds neck of male animal with ruffed neck which faces him. To the left he holds a second, rather schematic animal, which faces him with its head turned away. Below the man is a possible kneeling animal with outstretched, ruffed neck, facing right.
**Remarks:** Very worn and poorly executed. Traces of glaze on reverse.

## Registration No. 6581:02

**Dimensions:** Max. diam. 1.78, height 0.8.
**Profile:** Worn smooth.
**Reverse:** Worn smooth, probably originally button back.
**Location:** Building 60, Area 371. Floor.
**Design:** Black stone worn shapeless. No design or glaze visible.
**Remarks.** Possibly Persian Gulf Style.

## Registration No. 6583: 01

**Dimensions:** Max. diam. 3.01, height 1.21.
**Profile:** F2.
**Reverse:** Standard.
**Location:** Building 61, Area 610. Collapse.
**Design:** Two horned male animals facing a palm-frond. Each animal has a crescent above its back and a rosette/sun motif between its feet. Below them is a double-headed bull with ruffed necks, each head facing edge of seal.
**Remarks:** Pale-grey steatite.

## Registration No. 6672:04

**Dimensions:** Max. diam. 2.9, height 1.3.
**Profile:** N/A.
**Reverse:** Apex of shell, tip worn away to show hole.
**Location:** Building 67, Area 384. Collapse.
**Design:** Possible shell seal or counter. Natural spiral forms design.

## REGISTRATION No. 7001:29

Shell seal(?).
**Dimensions:** Max. diam. 5.5, height 1.2.
**Profile:** N/A.
**Reverse:** Apex of conch shell (Lambis Truncata).
**Location:** Building 34, Area 600. Collapse.
**Design:** Natural spiral forms design. Shell seal blank or counter.

## REGISTRATION No. 7008:5

**Dimensions:** Diam. 2.64, height 1.24.
**Profile** F1.
**Reverse:** Standard.
**Location:** Building 35, Area 604. Collapse.
**Design:** Recessed border with dog-tooth decoration, slightly damaged. In centre is rotating design of five long-horned animal heads, with long, ruffed necks, joined at the centre by a circle.
**Remarks:** Creamy steatite. Glazed.

## REGISTRATION No. 7533:01

**Dimensions:** Diam. 1.95, extant height 0.67.
**Profile:** F1(?).
**Reverse:** Standard.
**Location:** Building 35, Area 604. Occupation.
**Design:** Face of seal has flaked off exposing perforation which was drilled from both ends.
**Remarks:** Mottled stone with creamy surface.

## REGISTRATION No. 8028:01

**Dimensions:** Diam. 2.32, extant height 1.24.
**Profile:** F1, convex.
**Reverse:** Largely broken away, trace of one dot-and-circle motif.
**Location:** Building 353, Area 708. Midden.
**Design:** About one third of seal extant. One possible seated figure, facing left. Proto-Dilmun(?).
**Remarks:** Dark-grey stone.

## REGISTRATION No. E16:10:06

**Dimensions:** Diam. c.2.11, extant height 0.6, boss broken off.
**Profile:** F4.
**Reverse:** Boss missing, traces of three lines on periphery of seal. Perforation drilled from either end.
**Location:** Building 6, Area 24. Sand.
**Design:** Largely obliterated. Isolated drill holes extant, and traces of two long-necked animals facing each other.
**Remarks:** Reverse glazed.
**Museum No. 4821-2-90-3.**

## REGISTRATION No. E18:12:05

**Dimensions:** Diam. 2.67, height 1.0.
**Profile:** F1, convex.
**Reverse:** Badly worn, low boss, traces of three parallel lines but no evidence of dot-and-circle motifs.
**Location:** Building 1, Area 1. Occupation.
**Design:** Linear Style. A seated figure on the left, facing right, holding a pan balance, below which is a long-necked, round-bottomed jar on a stand. Second, much-damaged, standing figure with one arm raised, on the right.
**Remarks:** A similar pan balance comes from a grave of Early Dilmun date, and is on display in the National Museum of Bahrain. A pan balance is also shown on a sealing from Kültepe/Kanesh level II in the Syro–Cappadocian style (Teissier 1984, No. 532). Previously published Crawford 1991, p. 256, Fig. 3 and p. 259; Killick et al. 1991, p. 120, Fig. 12a. A little glaze remaining at base of boss.
**Museum No. 4135-3-90.**

## REGISTRATION No. E18:30:03

**Dimensions:** Diam. 2.60–2.70, height 1.24.
**Profile:** F2.
**Reverse:** Standard.
**Location:** Building 1, Area 1. Occupation.
**Design:** A standing human figure in a tiered skirt, facing right. In his left hand he holds a shield-like object, with spikes at the top and bottom. His right hand grasps the

hand of a second, naked, human figure, seated on a triangular stool, and also facing right. In the right field is an inverted, long-necked animal, with a broken, hatched rectangle above its back.
**Remarks:** Unusual, brownish stone speckled with pink. Reverse glazed. For design see Kjaerum 1983, No. 67. Previously published Crawford 1991, p. 259; Killick et al. 1991, p. 120, Fig. 12b.
**Museum No. 4132-3-90.**

## REGISTRATION No. F18:33:01

**Dimensions:** Diam. 2.1, height 1.86.
**Profile:** F2.
**Reverse:** Standard.
**Location:** Building 1, Area 2. Occupation.
**Design:** Two horned animals rampant on either side of a tree or branch. The long-horned animal on the left faces outwards, its neck stretched up and its head turned towards the tree. The short-horned animal on the right also faces out and turns its head towards the centre.
**Remarks:** Creamy stone with chip on one side. Traces of glaze, also on reverse. Previously published Crawford 1991, p. 259; Killick et al. 1991, p. 120, Fig. 12d.
**Museum No. 2986-3-90.**

## REGISTRATION No. F18:33:15

**Dimensions:** Diam. 2.2, extant height 0.9 (damaged).
**Profile:** F1, straight.
**Reverse:** Standard.
**Location:** Building 1, Area 2. Occupation.
**Design:** Two naked, standing, human figures facing left. The figure on the left holds a shield-like object to his

left, that on the right touches the head of an animal, on his right, with long, notched, back-swept horns. In his other hand he holds a jar. The animal faces left, and looks back over its shoulder to the edge of the seal. Between the heads of the two figures is a crescent with a possible sun above it.

**Remarks:** Very dark stone, glaze preserved in the figures. Previously published Crawford 1991, p. 260; Killick et al. 1991, p. 120, Fig. 12c.

**Museum No. 2991-3-90.**

## REGISTRATION No. F18:33:16

**Dimensions:** Diam. 2.61–2.67, height 1.56.
**Profile:** F2.
**Reverse:** Standard.
**Location:** Building 1, Area 2. Occupation.
**Design:** Two rampant horned animals, with their bodies crossing at the waist. Their heads are separated by a standard topped with a crescent. In the left field is a naked male figure, standing facing right, holding a spear. In the right field is a wedge-shaped motif, with an animal head and raised fore-limb protruding from the top. Between the animals' feet is an illegible motif, possibly a fish.

**Remarks:** Traces of glaze. Reverse also glazed. This seal shows elements of both Styles Ia and Ib. Previously published Crawford 1991, p. 260; Killick et al. 1991, p. 120, Fig. 12e.

**Museum No. 2988-3-90.**

## REGISTRATION No. G16:01:01

**Dimensions:** Diam. 2.0, extant height 1.0.
**Profile:** F3.
**Reverse:** Boss missing.
**Location:** Sand.
**Design:** Recessed border with incised lines around the inside. In left field is a naked, standing man, his right arm bent away from his body towards the border of the seal, while with the other hand he holds his erect penis. Above, and at right angles to him, is a very stylised female figure, facing right, legs wide apart, holding her feet in her hands, apparently engaged in sexual intercourse with the male. On either side of her head is a triangle, one hatched, the other probably originally hatched, but now damaged. Linear Style.

**Remarks:** Pale stone, with white glazed surface. Splitting, with two chips missing from the edge of the face.

**Museum No. 4816-2-90-3.**

## REGISTRATION No. G17:07:01

**Dimensions:** Diam. 1.11, height 0.96.
**Profile:** F1, straight.
**Reverse:** Standard.
**Location:** Building 4, Area 9. Occupation.
**Design:** A bearded figure wearing a hatched skirt, standing facing right, in a boat with an animal-head prow (damaged). He holds a shield-like object to the right, and to the left, a horned animal, with its head turned back over its shoulder to face left. In the right field is a plant motif, with a triangle above.

**Remarks:** Traces of glaze. Previously published Crawford 1991, p. 260.

**Museum No. 4134-3-90.**

## REGISTRATION No. G17:18:02

**Dimensions:** Diam. 2.70, height 1.25.
**Profile:** F2.
**Reverse:** Standard.
**Location:** Building 3, Area 5. Floor.
**Design:** A wheel of six animal heads joined at the base of their necks to a hatched central circle. Each animal has two horns and one possible ear shown. Four have straight horns and two are shown with curving horns. All face right. Two raised fore-legs are visible on one. Filler motifs between the heads are a hatched triangle, two wavy lines and a crescent.
**Remarks:** Traces of glaze. Reverse also glazed. This type of design is found over a wide area in the first half of the second millennium BC. A wheel of eight human figures is incorporated in a presentation scene in the Syrian style, dated c.1750–1620 BC (Teissier 1984, Nos. 453 and 557, showing a wheel of heroes). Other examples are known from Alalakh and Acemhöyük (Porada 1971). Previously published Crawford 1991, p. 260.
**Museum No. 2990-2-90.**

## REGISTRATION No. I14:20:10

Gable-backed rectangular seal.
**Dimensions:** 0.8 x 1.2 x 1.5.
**Profile:** Triangular.
**Reverse:** Standard, with the three lines across short axis of gable.
**Location:** Building 210, Area 206. Occupation.
**Design:** A couchant animal facing right, with a long, ruffed neck and upright horns. Above its back is a hatched square (4 x 7 squares).

**Remarks:** Very dark stone. No glaze. Previously published Crawford 1993, p. 9, Fig. 9.
**Museum No. 4817-2-90-3.**

## REGISTRATION No. K16:08:05

**Dimensions:** Diam. 2.4, height 1.20.
**Profile:** F2.
**Reverse:** Standard.
**Location:** Building 51, Area 55. Midden.
**Design:** Two short-horned animals facing outwards, looking back over their shoulders towards each other. Between them is a rectangular structure, partly hatched, possibly a door or altar. The top of the rectangle is decorated with a double-crescent standard. Drilled motifs in each of the two upper crescents.
**Remarks:** Traces of glaze. Reverse also glazed. Previously published Crawford 1991, p. 261.
**Museum No. 4136-3-90.**

## REGISTRATION No. K16:29:03

**Dimensions:** Diam. 2.03, height 0.96.
**Profile:** F4, grooved? (worn).
**Reverse:** Standard with lines worn away at apex of dome.
**Location:** Building 51, Area 55. Floor.
**Design:** Five standing bearded figures, with long skirts and narrow waists, all facing right and holding hands. Above the central figure is a crescent moon on its back, with a six-pointed star on either side of it.
**Remarks:** Traces of glaze. Compare Kjaerum 1983, Nos. 190–192.
**Museum No. 4814-2-90-3.**

## REGISTRATION NO. K16:29:08

**Dimensions:** Diam. 2.47, extant height 0.75.
**Profile:** F2.
**Reverse:** Damaged.
**Location:** Building 51, Area 55. Floor.
**Design:** A naked female figure is seen from the front with legs wide apart, head turned to the right. To the left of her head is a turtle or lizard; to the right is a second, unidentified, motif. Below her, at right angles to her legs, is a male figure, head missing, holding his erect penis in his right hand, apparently about to enter her. In his left hand he holds a straw coming from a jar at his feet.
**Remarks:** Stamp seals showing female figures in similar positions have a long tradition in Susa and in Anshan where they are often made of a bituminous compound (Amiet 1986, p. 267). Previously published Crawford 1991, p. 261.
**Museum No. 4815-2-90-3.**

## REGISTRATION NO. K16:29:13

**Dimensions:** Diam. 0.9, height 1.75.
**Profile:** F2.
**Reverse:** Standard.
**Location:** Building 51, Area 55. Floor.
**Design:** A deeply-incised, schematic design. In the centre a snake is shown as a vertical zigzag with a beak-like head. To either side of the snake a stylized human figure with outstretched arms appears to be dancing. In the right field is a hatched motif, perhaps a fish.
**Remarks:** An unusual style.
**Museum No. 4815-2-90-3.**

## REGISTRATION NO. K16:29:16

**Dimensions:** Diam. 0.98, height 2.33.
**Profile:** F1, convex, but worn.
**Reverse:** Standard, worn over apex of boss.
**Location:** Building 51, Area 55. Floor.
**Design:** Four horned animals, three of them around the edge of the seal, two of which face outwards, the middle one with its head to the centre. A fourth animal, with an elongated, ruffed neck, stands above it, and has its head to the edge of the seal.
**Remarks:** Traces of glaze, also on reverse.
**Museum No. 4819-2-90-3.**

## REGISTRATION NO. K16:53:10

**Dimensions:** Diam. 2.65, height 1.15.
**Profile:** F1, convex, worn.
**Reverse:** Standard but worn over apex. Traces of glaze.
**Location:** Building 51, Area 56. Make-up.
**Design:** A central, standing figure in a tiered skirt, facing right, torso in profile, with hands raised towards a horned male animal, which faces left but looks back over its shoulder towards a crescent in the right field. To the left of the standing figure is a second, horned, male animal, facing left, with its head turned back towards the central figure. Below this is a damaged foot motif.
**Remarks:** The seal is worn and the style shows elements of both Kjaerum's Styles Ia and Ib.
**Museum No. 4818-2-90-3.**

## REGISTRATION No. L18:27:07

**Dimensions:** Diam. 1.8, extant height 0.7.
**Profile:** F4, grooved.
**Reverse:** High boss, broken and worn. No decoration visible.
**Location:** Building 53, Area 61. Make-up.
**Design:** Linear Style. Difficult to interpret. Probably shows schematic, long-horned animal facing right, with a possible second horned animal, also facing right. Along the edge, above the horns of the second animal, is a curved line with left end thickened. An irregular line is seen above the back of the second animal, at right angles to the first, above its back. Two curved lines in upper right field, and a triangular mark in left field.
**Remarks:** Persian Gulf Style. Unusual mottled green stone. No glaze, no use of drill.
**Museum No. 2810-90-3.**

## REGISTRATION No. P19:01:10

**Dimensions:** Diam. 2.60–2.64, height 1.32.
**Profile:** F2.
**Reverse:** Standard.
**Location:** Building 100, Area 101. Occupation.
**Design:** Central divine figure, seated facing right, on stool, wearing horned head-dress and tiered skirt; holds in one hand a long straw, through which he is drinking out of a pot set at his feet. Below him is a scorpion facing left. In front of him, and facing him, is a kneeling gazelle above damaged bird motif. An unidentified symbol lies above the gazelle's head. Behind the seated figure is a smaller, naked, standing figure, facing and touching the seated figure with one hand. In the other he holds a crescentic object with a hatched triangle at

one end. Below this is an offering stand, above which is a rosette or sun.
**Remarks:** Reverse glazed. Previously published Crawford 1991, p. 261 and Crawford & Matthews 1997, p. 90, Fig. 88.
**Museum No. 2989-3-90.**

## REGISTRATION No. Q20:22:07

Shell seal.
**Dimensions:** Max. diam. 3.5, height 1.4.
**Profile:** F2.
**Reverse:** Perforated through centre, traces of burning on raised central area.
**Location:** Building 104, Area 113. Floor.
**Design:** Spiral formed by transverse cut through shell.

All dimensions are in centimetres. Where a measurement or detail of description is lacking, it was not available at time of writing.
It appears that, in the vast majority of cases, the impressions are from round, stamp-seals.
Sealings found in the temple have been previously published (Crawford & Matthews 1997) and are not included here.

## REGISTRATION No. 1021:03

**Dimensions:** 2.5 x 2.4 x 1.0.
**Reverse:** Knot-impression.
**Location:** Building 211, Area 212. Oven fill.
**Description:** Yellow/green clay. Area of smoothed edge present. **Obverse:** Seated stick figure on the right. Another figure (damaged), on the left, drinks from a pot at his feet, through a straw held in one hand. A human foot is visible in the centre, with a vertical line to its right. From the same seal as 1021:4 and 5(?). Linear Style. Estimated diam. of seal 2.2.

## REGISTRATION No. 1021:04

**Dimensions:** 1.9 x 2.0 x 0.3.
**Reverse:** Broken away.
**Location:** Building 211, Area 212. Oven fill.
**Description:** Yellow/green clay. **Obverse:** Seated figure on the right, and part of fragmentary figure on left holding a drinking straw which goes to a pot at his feet. Possibly from the same seal as 1021:3 and 5, and similar to 1856:01

## REGISTRATION No. 1021:05

**Dimensions:** 2.4 x 2.2 x 0.6.
**Reverse:** String-impressions.
**Location:** Building 211, Area 212. Oven fill.

**Description:** Gritty, grey clay with white inclusions, burnt. Small section of smoothed edge. **Obverse:** Very worn impression. Seated figure to left drinking from straw which goes to a jar at his feet. Possibly from the same seal as 1021:3 and 4, similar to 1856:05.

## REGISTRATION No. 1021:06

**Dimensions:** 2.0 x 1.3 x 0.9.
**Reverse:** String-impression/knot.
**Location:** Building 211, Area 212. Oven fill.
**Description:** Yellow/green clay, with inclusions. Badly worn, traces of rim of circular seal, motifs illegible, on obverse.

## REGISTRATION No. 1021:07

**Dimensions:** 1.6 x 1.2 x 0.2.
**Reverse:** Faint string-impression.
**Location:** Building 211, Area 212. Oven fill.
**Description:** Pinkish clay, baked. **Obverse:** Fragmentary seal impression. Possible animal head and an incised line.

## REGISTRATION No. 1021:08

Two fragments
**Dimensions:** (i) 15 x 1.0 x 0.6. (ii) 2.1 x 1.2 x 0.6.
**Reverse:** Both fragments have impressions, possibly of wood.
**Location:** Building 211, Area 212. Oven fill.
**Description:** Yellow/green clay with crystalline inclusions. Larger piece has one smoothed surface with finger-prints, smaller has finger-prints on smoothed edge.

## REGISTRATION No. 1024:04

**Dimensions:** 2.1 x 1.3 x 1.5.
**Reverse:** String-impression.
**Location:** Building 210, Area 207. Occupation.
**Description:** Hardened yellow/green clay.
**Obverse:** Naked human figure with bent arm outstretched towards a horizontally-striped object, which has a possible leg or claw at the bottom near the figure's legs.

## REGISTRATION NO. 1024:17

**Dimensions:** 2.2 x 1.5 x 0.6.
**Reverse:** Impression of string or knot.
**Location:** Building 210, Area 207. Occupation.
**Description:** Yellow/green hardened clay. Segment of lower third of seal with smoothed edge distorted by pressure. Finger-print visible.
**Obverse (from right):** Lower part of a possible shield, the legs of a human figure facing left, a much-damaged second figure, and part of a hatched rectangle.

## REGISTRATION NO. 1024:22

Four fragments.
**Dimensions:** (i) 1.9 x 1.6 x 1.0. (ii) 1.7 x 1.2 x 1.1.
(iii) 1.8 x 1.4 x 0.8. (iv) 1.8 x 1.1 x 0.4.
**Reverse:** Largest piece has knot-and-string-impression, the rest string.
**Location:** Building 210, Area 207. Occupation.
**Description:** Three pieces of greenish grey clay, one of pink clay. Largest has deep finger-print on obverse. Two have the impression of the edge of a seal but design illegible.

## REGISTRATION NO. 1025:04

**Dimensions:** 1.4 x 1.23 x 1.2.
**Reverse:** String-impression.
**Location:** Building 210, Area 206. Floor.
**Description:** Sandy, grey clay. Worn design shows lower part of a standing figure in a long skirt, holding a straw in a pot to the right.

## REGISTRATION NO. 1029:01

**Dimensions:** 1.7 x 1.45 x 0.95.
**Reverse:** Knot-impression.
**Location:** Building 210, Area 207. Pit fill.
**Description:** Yellow/green hardened clay. Irregular shape.
**Obverse:** Body of a male animal, triangular indentation above his back.

## REGISTRATION NO. 1029:02.

**Dimensions:** 2.6 x 2.8 x 1.2.
**Reverse:** Smooth, convex surface, with a string-hole at one edge. Perforation does not go through. This suggests use as a tag or label with end of string embedded in it.
**Location:** Building 210, Area 207. Pit fill.
**Description:** Hemispherical piece of hard, baked, red/orange clay. Made the same size as the seal used on it, so it has a seal impression exactly fitting the flat surface.
**Obverse:** A standing figure in a long skirt. To the left of the figure is a scorpion. To the right is a horned animal, looking back over its shoulder at the human figure.

## REGISTRATION NO. 1029:03

**Dimensions:** 2.5 x 2.2 x 1.1.
**Reverse:** String-impression.
**Location:** Building 210, Area 207. Pit fill.
**Description:** One edge flattened and smooth.
**Obverse:** Design largely eroded, no legible motifs.

## REGISTRATION NO. 1029:04

**Dimensions:** 1.6 x 0.9 x 1.3.
**Reverse:** Possible string-impression.
**Location:** Building 210, Area 207. Pit fill.
**Description:** Small area of sealing on light-grey, hardened clay, one smoothed edge with finger-print.
**Obverse:** No legible motifs.

## REGISTRATION NO. 1029:05

**Dimensions:** 2.0 x 1.3 x 1.0.
**Reverse:** Tubular impression, perhaps of peg, or rim of pot.
**Location:** Building 210, Area 207. Pit fill.
**Description:** Yellow/green hardened clay. Centre of seal impression, one smoothed edge with finger-print.

**Obverse:** Seated, nude, human figure facing left, arms outstretched, his feet above back of damaged animal. Illegible motif in upper right field.

### REGISTRATION No. 1029:06
**Dimensions:** 1.8 x 1.3 x 0.5.
**Reverse:** String-impression.
**Location:** Building 210, Area 207. Pit fill.
**Description:** Yellow/green clay.
**Obverse:** Smooth. Arc of part of edge of seal visible.

### REGISTRATION No. 1029:07
**Dimensions:** 1.8 x 1.3 x 0.5.
**Reverse:** Possible string-impressions. Finger-print.
**Location:** Building 210, Area 207. Pit fill.
**Description:** Piece of hardened, yellow/green clay, probably a sealing. Obverse has impression of something flat and striated, e.g. wood. Irregular in shape.

### REGISTRATION No. 1029:08
**Dimensions:** 1.7 x 1.2 x 1.1.
**Location:** Building 210, Area 207. Pit fill.
**Reverse:** Parallel impressions of thin strips (perhaps of palm-leaf).
**Description:** Piece of hardened, yellow/green clay pinched into roughly triangular shape with smooth surfaces. No design visible.

### REGISTRATION No. 1029:09
**Dimensions:** 2.0 x 0.8 x 0.8.
**Reverse:** Not described.
**Location:** Building 210, Area 207. Pit fill.
**Description:** Piece of clay with impression of the edge of a seal. Two surfaces seem to be smoothed, but no remaining design is visible.

### REGISTRATION No. 1029:10
**Dimensions:** 1.1 x 1.0 x 0.9.
**Reverse:** Surface missing.
**Location:** Building 210, Area 207. Pit fill.
**Description:** Hardened grey clay, roughly triangular, one broken surface. No design visible.

### REGISTRATION No. 1029:11
**Dimensions:** 1.5 x 0.6 x 0.4.
**Reverse:** Surface missing.
**Location:** Building 210, Area 207. Pit fill.
**Description:** Oblong fragment of hardened, pale-grey clay. One surface smoothed.

### REGISTRATION No. 1029:12
**Dimensions:** 1.3 x 0.6 x 0.4.
**Reverse:** String-impression.
**Location:** Building 210, Area 207. Pit fill.
**Description:** Irregular fragment of hardened grey clay. One surface smoothed.

### REGISTRATION No. 1029:13
**Dimensions:** 1.1 x 0.5 x 0.4.
**Reverse:** Surface missing.
**Location:** Building 210, Area 207. Pit fill.
**Description:** Fragment of pale-grey clay, one surface smoothed. No design visible.

### REGISTRATION No. 1029:14
**Dimensions:** 1.0 x 0.9 x 0.4.
**Reverse:** Not described.
**Location:** Building 210, Area 207. Pit fill.
**Description:** Hardened, grey clay. Part of seal impression remaining on one surface. Two lines at right angles, with one wavy line, possibly the horns of an animal.

### REGISTRATION No. 1041:01
**Dimensions:** 2.2 x 1.2 x 1.0.
**Reverse:** Possible string-impression.
**Location:** Building 211, Area 212. Collapse.
**Description:** Yellow/green, hardened clay. Badly eroded and irregular in shape.
**Obverse:** Hatched strip, possibly part of hatched cross(?).

## REGISTRATION No. 1041:17

**Dimensions:** 3.2 x 2.3 x 1.8.
**Reverse:** Impressions of knot and string.
**Location:** Building 211, Area 212. Occupation.
**Description:** Irregular fragment of yellow/green, hardened clay with white inclusions.
**Obverse:** Damaged. There appears to be a palm-tree in the centre with illegible motifs on either side.

## REGISTRATION No. 1041:18

**Dimensions:** 1.7 x 1.3 x 0.8.
**Reverse:** Possible string-impression.
**Location:** Building 211, Area 212. Occupation.
**Description:** Fragment of grey clay with deeply impressed edge of seal. Design illegible.

## REGISTRATION No. 1041:19

**Dimensions:** 1.7 x 1.2 x 0.5.
**Reverse:** String-impression.
**Location:** Building 211, Area 212. Occupation.
**Description:** Fragment of yellow/green clay, with small area of smoothed edge. **Obverse:** Badly damaged human figure with arm raised to left. Rosette below raised arm.

## REGISTRATION No. 1041:20

(Not described).

## REGISTRATION No. 1042:01

**Dimensions:** 1.8 x 1.4 x 0.9.
**Reverse:** No impression.
**Location:** Building 211, Area 211. Floor.
**Description:** Fragment of yellow/green hardened clay, approximately semicircular, with small area of smoothed edge. **Obverse:** The upper torso and head of a man facing right. In his raised hand he appears to be holding the nose of a short-horned animal, which faces him. The head, abdomen and left fore-leg of the animal can be seen.

## REGISTRATION No. 1042:16

**Dimensions:** 2.2 x 1.5 x 0.7.
**Reverse:** Two parallel string-impressions and a smoothed area.
**Location:** Building 211, Area 211. Floor.
**Description:** Fragment of yellow/green clay.
**Obverse:** Badly worn. Damaged animal body, and traces of legs at right angles to it.

## REGISTRATION No. 1042:17

**Dimensions:** 2.6 x 1.8 x 0.8.
**Reverse:** Faint string-impression.
**Location:** Building 211, Area 211. Floor.
**Description:** Two fragments of yellow/green clay, badly eroded. **Obverse:** A horned animal looking back over its shoulder to the left. Below is a possible second animal. To its right a possible human figure, holding the first animal by the horns. The remainder is too badly eroded to identify.

## REGISTRATION No. 1042:18

**Dimensions:** 1.8 x 2.1 x 0.75.
**Reverse:** Knot-impression.
**Location:** Building 211, Area 211. Floor.
**Description:** Light-grey, hardened clay. Virtually-complete impression. Estimated diam. of seal 1.7. **Obverse:** Two horned animals, rampant, one on either side of a turtle or

tortoise. A rosette or star is in the field above the head of the tortoise. Found in association with a cooking-pot (1042:14). From the same seal as 1042:19, 20, 21 and 22. Previously published Woodburn & Crawford 1994, p. 103, Fig. 21.

## REGISTRATION No. 1042:19

**Dimensions:** 2.2 x 2.4 x 0.75.
**Reverse:** Parallel string-impressions.
**Location:** Building 211, Area 211. Floor.
**Description:** Light-grey, hardened clay. Virtually-complete circular impression, with areas of smoothed edge. Diam. of seal 1.7. The very well-defined design is identical to that on 1042:18, 20, 21 and 22. Found in association with cooking pot 1042:14.

## REGISTRATION No. 1042:20

**Dimensions:** 1.2 x 1.9 x 0.7.
**Reverse:** Knot-impression.
**Location:** Building 211, Area 211. Floor.
**Description:** Yellow/green clay.
**Obverse:** A turtle or tortoise between the lower limbs of two rampant animals with horns. This is the same design that appears on fragments 1042:18, 19, 21 and 22. Found in association with cooking pot 1042:14.

## REGISTRATION No. 1042:21

**Dimensions:** 1.9 x 1.8 x 1.0.
**Reverse:** Deep string-impression.
**Location:** Building 211, Area 211. Floor.
**Description:** Light-grey clay with about three-quarters of a seal impression remaining.
**Obverse:** Poor definition, but seems to be identical to fragments 1042:18, 19, 20 and 22. Turtle or tortoise, and star visible. Found in association with cooking pot 1042:14.

## REGISTRATION No. 1042:22

**Dimensions:** 2.1 x 0.9 x 0.7.
**Reverse:** Worn.
**Location:** Building 211, Area 211. Floor.
**Description:** Light-grey, rectangular fragment. Badly worn on both sides. **Obverse:** Upper bodies of two horned animals, with turtle or tortoise between them, the same design as seen on 1042:18, 19, 20 and 21. Found in association with cooking pot 1042:14.

## REGISTRATION No. 1042:23

**Dimensions:** 2.0 x 1.6 x 0.7.
**Reverse:** Worn.
**Location:** Building 211, Area 211. Floor.
**Description:** Yellow/green clay. **Obverse:** The upper right quadrant of a circular seal impression, a seated monkey-like creature on the right, facing left towards a short-horned animal. Below them is the head and neck of a possible bull.

## REGISTRATION No. 1042:24
**Dimensions:** 3.0 x 2.0 x 0.8.
**Reverse:** Surface missing.
**Location:** Building 211, Area 211. Floor.
**Description:** Very poor condition.

## REGISTRATION No. 1042:26

**Dimensions:** 2.1 x 1.7 x 0.7.
**Reverse:** Possible impression of peg(?).
Estimated diam. of peg 0.6.
**Location:** Building 211, Area 211. Floor.

**Description:** Yellow/green clay fragment, with one smooth surface, at approximately eighty degrees to obverse. **Obverse:** Double line of a long, hatched area, perhaps a net (7–8 squares visible), with two filled squares either side of a line running at right angles to the net.

## REGISTRATION No. 1045:01

**Dimensions:** 1.8 x 1.3 x 0.8.
**Reverse:** Deep string-impression.
**Location:** Building 211, Area 212. Floor.
**Description:** Dark-greenish clay. Virtually-complete impression. one smoothed edge. Estimated diam. of seal 1.9. **Obverse:** A standing male figure in a skirt, facing right, arms held out to either side. To the right he touches the neck of a horned animal, which looks back over its shoulder at the man. A palm-frond or branch appears in the field between the man and animal.

## REGISTRATION No. 1045:03

**Dimensions:** 1.6 x 1.5 x 1.1 (largest fragment).
**Reverse:** Traces of string-impressions.
**Location:** Building 211, Area 212. Floor.
**Description:** Six small fragments of light-grey, sandy clay.

## REGISTRATION No. 1051:06

**Dimensions:** 2.2 x 1.3 x 0.5.
**Reverse:** String-impressions.
**Location:** Building 211, Area 214. Collapse.
**Description:** Grey clay. **Obverse:** No coherent design visible, two lines apparently forming a V-shape.

## REGISTRATION No. 1067:06

**Dimensions:** 2.2 x 1.7 x 1.0 (largest fragment).
**Reverse:** Not described.
**Location:** Building 211, Area 212. Floor.
**Description:** Fourteen fragments of light-green, sandy clay, possibly sealings. Much-damaged. No design discernible.

## REGISTRATION No. 1087:06

Three fragments.
(i) 1.4 x 1.2 x 0.4. (ii) 1.2 x 0.9 x 0.9. (iii) 0.8 x 0.6 x 0.7.
**Reverse:** (i) String-impression and cloth.
(ii) Cloth impression. (iii) String-impression.
**Location:** Building 50, Area 91. Collapse.
**Description:** Light khaki-green clay. (i) Obverse eroded, one smooth surface. (ii) Smooth surface with possible animal head. (iii) No design visible. Cloth and string-impressions suggest fragments of a jar sealing.

## REGISTRATION No. 1093:04

**Dimensions:** 1.3 x 0.9 x 0.8.
**Reverse:** Surface missing.
**Location:** Building 50, Area 90. Collapse.
**Description:** Very light green, sandy clay. Indentation on one side with parallel ridges. No design visible.

## REGISTRATION No. 1101:07

Three fragments.
**Dimensions:** (i) 1.6 x 1.1 x 0.6. (ii) 1.1 x1.3 x 0.9.
(iii) 0.95 x 0.55 x 0.5.
**Reverse:** Surfaces missing.
**Location:** Building 50, Area 90. Collapse.
**Description:** Light-green, sandy clay. (ii) and (iii) each have one smoothed surface.

## REGISTRATION No. 1105:02

Four fragments.
**Dimensions:** (i) 2.35 x 1.6 x 0.7.
(ii) 2.0 x 0.95 x 0.45. (iii) 2.0 x 1.4 x 0.9. (iv) 1.0 x 0.8 x 0.4.
**Reverse:** (i) Flat and smooth, with tubular, pencil-shaped hole through body. (ii) Flat, smooth area. (iii) and (iv) No impressions.
**Location:** Building 50, Area 90. Floor.
**Description:** Fine, grey clay. (i) Two fragments glued together. About one-third of impression including left edge of seal. **Obverse:** a schematic horned animal, standing facing left. Above its back is a rosette or sun, and to the left is a vertical motif. From a Proto-Dilmun seal, as the head of the animal appears drawn not drilled.
(ii) **Obverse:** left edge of impression from same seal as (i), showing fore-part of animal and the vertical motif.
No design on (iii) and (iv).

## REGISTRATION No. 1108:02

**Description:** Fragments of clay, apparently bearing seal impression. No further description.

## REGISTRATION No. 1117:04

Two fragments.
**Dimensions:** (i) 1.7 x 1.8 x 0.9. (ii) 2.3 x 2.0 x 0.8.
**Reverse:** Surface missing.
**Location:** Building 200, Area 205. Floor.
**Description:** Light-grey clay with salt crystals.
(i) Impression of right-angled edge.

## REGISTRATION No. 1131:09

**Dimensions:** 1.0 x 1.3 x 0.4.
**Reverse:** String-impressions.
**Location:** Building 200, Area 205. Make-up.
**Description:** Fine, light-grey clay.

**Obverse:** Upper left segment of an impression, the head of bearded figure looking left, sharply defined. In front of the face is the end of a pointed object, while on the left edge is another very damaged motif. See also 1161:04 for reconstruction of entire design and list of sealings apparently from same seal.

## REGISTRATION No. 1133:06

**Dimensions:** 2.6 x 1.5 x 0.8 (largest fragment).
**Reverse:** String-marks and smooth areas.
**Location:** Building 211, Area 212. Make-up.
**Description:** Fourteen fragments of light-grey, sandy clay with white inclusions. One fragment has smoothed edge, with rosette visible on obverse, and other illegible motifs.

## REGISTRATION No. 1133:14

 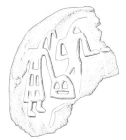

**Dimensions:** 2.5 x 1.9 x 0.9.
**Reverse:** Knot-impression.
**Location:** Building 211, Area 212. Make-up.

**Description:** Fine, yellowish clay. **Obverse:** Design distorted, with about half extant. On left edge is standing figure in tiered skirt, holding a curious bag-like object to the right, and facing a second naked figure, head missing, both arms bent at the waist, and pointing to the right. Second, bag-like motif below his waist.

## REGISTRATION No. 1133:15

**Dimensions:** 2.2 x 2.4 x 1.5.
**Reverse:** Knot-impression.
**Location:** Building 211, Area 212. Make-up.
**Description:** Slightly-sandy, grey clay with salt crystals.
**Obverse:** Design badly worn. Seated figure on left, damaged, looking right, towards short-horned male animal, perhaps a bull, with legs tucked under it, also looking right. Indecipherable motifs over its back and below head. Estimated diam. of seal 2.2.

## REGISTRATION No. 1133:17

**Dimensions:** 2.2 x 2.67 x 0.8.
**Reverse:** Knot-impression.
**Location:** Building 211, Area 212. Make-up.
**Description:** Slightly-sandy, grey clay with salt crystals. Badly damaged, two joining fragments.

**Obverse:** Possible traces of hatched square, with necks of two animals protruding from top corners, a V-shaped symbol between them.

## REGISTRATION No. 1136:07

**Dimensions:** 1.5 x 2.5 x 1.0.
**Reverse:** String-marks.
**Location:** Building 211, Area 212. Floor.
**Description:** Sandy, grey clay. Triangular fragment of a clay disk. Broken edges with finger-print. **Obverse:** Seated, nude, male figure looking left towards gazelle, legs broken off. Gazelle looks back towards edge of seal.

## REGISTRATION No. 1154:01

**Dimensions:** 1.55 x 1.42 x 0.43.
**Reverse:** String-impressions.
**Location:** Building 211,
Area 211. Threshold.
**Description:** Dark-grey, burnt clay,
one smoothed edge.
**Obverse:** Hatched rectangle (7 x 4 squares).
Traces of three objects protruding from one narrow side.

## REGISTRATION No. 1158:15

**Dimensions:** 2.55 x 0.9 x 0.6.
**Reverse:** String(?).
**Location:** Building 211,
Area 212. Make-up.
**Description:** Fine, light-grey clay. Smoothed edge.
**Obverse:** Possible necks of two horned animals, perhaps
originally protruding from hatched square.

## REGISTRATION No. 1159:08

**Dimensions:** 1.3 x 1.45 x 0.7.
**Reverse:** Slightly-convex and smoothed.
**Location:** Building 200, Area 204. Floor.
**Description:** Fine, pinkish clay with inclusions.
Impressions of leaves or wood on one flat surface.

## REGISTRATION No. 1161:04

**Dimensions:** 2.0 x 1.5 x 0.94.
**Reverse:** Knot-impression.
**Location:** Building 211,
Area 212. Floor.
**Description:** Fine, light-grey clay.
Left edge and part of the lower edge of
impression. **Obverse:** Standing,
bearded figure, head missing, in three-
tiered net skirt, facing left towards a seated monkey-like
figure facing right. Between them is a jar on a stand, with
a drinking straw protruding from it; both figures hold the
straw. From same seal as 1161:05, 09, 14, 15, 1131:09
and 5176:01.
**Reconstructed design:** Central, standing, bearded figure, in
a long net skirt, with raised arms facing left, and both feet
showing below hem of skirt. To left is seated, monkey-like
figure (see Kjaerum 1983, Nos.107 and 137) and between
them is a possible jar on a two-legged pot-stand, with a
straw in it. To right of figure (design broken), part of human
figure with head in profile, apparently holding a palm-frond.

## REGISTRATION No. 1161:05

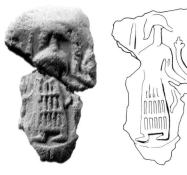

**Dimensions:** 2.9 x 1.6 x 1.05.
**Reverse:** Possible impression of small peg.
**Location:** Building 211, Area 212. Floor.
**Description:** Light-grey, fine clay. Estimated diam. of seal:
2.3. **Obverse:** Standing, bearded figure with three-tiered
net skirt, facing left, feet below skirt. End of drinking
straw visible in front of his face. To the right, head and
arm of second figure looking left and holding palm-frond.
Joined to 1161:10. See also 1161: 04 for reconstruction
of seal design and list of other sealings with same design.

## REGISTRATION No. 1161:09

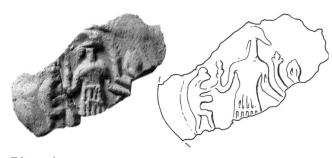

**Dimensions:** 3.0 x 1.37 x 1.15.
**Reverse:** Knot-impression.
**Location:** Building 211, Area 212. Floor.
**Description:** Fine, light-grey clay. Part of smoothed edge
with finger-prints. Most of the upper half of a seal
impression. **Obverse:** Standing, bearded figure facing left,
two tiers of skirt remaining. To left is seated, monkey-like
creature, drinking straw and pot between them. To the
right is second (broken) figure, facing left, and holding a
palm-frond. See also 1161: 04 for reconstruction of seal
design and list of other sealings with same design.

## REGISTRATION No. 1161:10

Now joined to 1161:05 (q.v).

## REGISTRATION No. 1161:11

**Dimensions:** 1.8 x 1.4 x 1.1 (largest fragment).
**Reverse:** Impressions of string, and of tubular object.
**Location:** Building 211, Area 212. Floor.
**Description:** Five fragments of very friable light-grey clay. No impressions.

## REGISTRATION No. 1161:14

**Dimensions:** 1.35 x 1.54 x 0.8.
**Reverse:** Surface missing.
**Location:** Building 211, Area 212. Floor.
**Description:** Fine, light-grey clay, one inclusion visible. **Obverse:** Bottom left of a seal impression. Lowest tier of net skirt with one foot facing left, while to left is pot on stand. See also 1161:04 for reconstruction of seal design and list of other sealings with the same design.

## REGISTRATION No. 1161:15

**Dimensions:** 1.8 x 1.4 x 0.75.
**Reverse:** String-impressions.
**Location:** Building 211, Area 212. Floor.
**Description:** Fine, light-grey clay. One smoothed edge.

**Obverse:** Top left quadrant of a seal impression. Head and torso of bearded figure, facing left towards head and torso of seated monkey-like creature. Both hold a drinking straw between them. Edge of seal clearly visible. See also 1161:04 for reconstruction of seal design and list of other sealings with same design.

## REGISTRATION No. 1573:01

**Dimensions:** Not measured
**Reverse:** No impression.
**Location:** Building 203, Area 202. Feature.
**Description: Obverse:** Body and hind-legs of an animal, perhaps a gazelle. Possibly part of a tag.

## REGISTRATION No. 1580:03

**Dimensions:** 2.0 x 1.6 x 0.9.
**Reverse:** Possible knot-impression.
**Location:** Building 203, Area 229. Occupation.
**Description:** Fragment in yellow/green clay. One smoothed edge with finger-prints. **Obverse:** Worn.

## REGISTRATION No. 1580:05

**Dimensions:** 1.4 x 1.0 x 0.7.
**Reverse:** No impression.
**Location:** Building 203, Area 229. Occupation.
**Description:** Fragment of grey clay. **Obverse:** A horned animal with a long, ruffed neck; above it and at right angles to it, a pair of possible animal legs facing right. In front of the legs is an unidentified motif.

## REGISTRATION No. 1622:02

**Dimensions:** 2.3 x 2.2 x 1.0.
**Reverse:** Parallel string-impressions and smooth edge. Jar sealing(?).
**Location:** Building 203, Area 229.
From cooking pot 1622:11.
**Description:** Pale-yellowish clay. Two smoothed edges with finger-prints. **Obverse:** Body of male animal, perhaps a bull, with ruffed neck, standing or running. Illegible motifs above its back.

## REGISTRATION No. 1622:03

**Dimensions:** 2.4 x 1.6 x 1.0.
**Reverse:** String-impression through body. One side has impressions of parallel pieces of leaf and shows a seam between two sets of parallel impressions. These impressions are of some kind of woven or plaited material.
**Location:** Building 203, Area 229.
From cooking pot 1622:11.
**Description:** Hard, gritty, grey clay. There is no seal impression.

### REGISTRATION No. 1622:04

**Dimensions:** 1.6 x 1.3 x 0.6.
**Reverse:** Worn knot-impression.
**Location:** Building 203, Area 229.
From cooking pot 1622:11.
**Description:** Gritty, light-brown clay.
**Obverse:** Two lines at right angles,
probably part of a cross dividing the seal into four
quadrants. Surviving quadrant shows a crab, and another
just visible in the opposing quadrant. Apparently from the
same seal as 1622:6, 7 and 8.

### REGISTRATION No. 1622:05

**Dimensions:** 1.3 x 1.1 x 0.8.
**Reverse:** Possible string-impression.
**Location:** Building 203, Area 229.
From cooking pot 1622:11.
**Description:** Fragment of yellowish clay,
small area of smooth edge.
**Obverse:** Fragmentary motifs from deeply incised,
linear-style seal, perhaps a curly tail on left and the rump
of an animal to the right.

### REGISTRATION No. 1622:06

**Dimensions:** (i) 1.8 x 0.9 x 0.7. (ii) 0.4 x 1.3 x 1.0.
**Reverse:** String-impressions on each, flat surface on larger
piece. Jar sealing(?).
**Location:** Building 203, Area 229.
From cooking pot 1611:11.
**Description:** Dark-grey, burnt clay. Area of smoothed edge
on larger piece. **Obverse:** (i) one quarter of seal impression
showing two arms of an incised cross with a crab in the
angle between them. From the same seal as 1622:4, 7 and
8. (ii) No impression. Drawing is reconstruction of
complete design, based on all related fragments.

### REGISTRATION No. 1622:07

**Dimensions:** 2.6 x 1.7 x 1.4.
**Reverse:** Two deep, parallel, string-impressions.
**Location:** Building 203, Area 229.
From cooking pot 1622:11.
**Description:** Gritty, yellowish clay. A small area of
smoothed edge. Incomplete design divided into quadrants
by incised lines. A crab is visible in each of the two
almost-complete quadrants. The others are broken away.
From same seal as 1622:4, 6 and 8.

### REGISTRATION No. 1622:08

**Dimensions:** 2.0 x 1.4 x 0.8.
**Reverse:** String-impressions.
**Location:** Building 203, Area 229.
From cooking pot 1622:11.
**Description:** Hard, gritty, yellowish
clay. Broken area of smoothed
edge. Obverse: Distorted, design
divided by incised lines into quadrants, two of which
survive. One contains a crab, another part of a crab.
From the same seal as 1622:4, 6 and 7.

### REGISTRATION No. 1733:01

**Dimensions:** 1.4 x 1.1 x 0.5.
**Reverse:** Faint string-impressions.
**Location:** Building 203, Area 229. Occupation.
**Description:** Light-green and grey, sandy clay.
Top surface smooth, no design visible.

### REGISTRATION No. 1771:01

**Dimensions:** 1.8 x 2.65 x 1.1.
**Reverse:** Two parallel lines of string-impressions.
**Location:** Building 204, Area 233. Floor.
**Description:** Light-grey clay with inclusions. One smoothed
edge. **Obverse:** Badly worn. Torso of human figure facing
right, with other illegible motifs to the right.

## REGISTRATION No. 1853:21

**Dimensions:** 2.1 x 1.8 x 1.6 (largest fragment).
**Reverse:** Surface missing.
**Location:** Building 207, Area 272, Square 25. Occupation.
**Description:** Half of spherical sealing or bead of soft, dark-grey clay, very friable, in three pieces. Originally perforated. At one point there are faint impressions, perhaps of straw.

## REGISTRATION No. 1853:47

**Dimensions:** 1.0 x 0.7 x 0.4.
**Reverse:** Two parallel string-impressions.
**Location:** Building 207, Area 272, Square 24. Occupation.
**Description:** Grey clay, with flecks of white.
**Obverse:** Possible pair of human feet.

## REGISTRATION No. 1853:95

**Dimensions:** 2.3 x 1.2 x 1.1.
**Reverse:** String-impressions.
**Location:** Building 207, Area 272, Square 26. Occupation.
**Description:** Semicircular sealing. Grey clay with traces of burning; small shells visible. One edge preserved, with finger-prints on it. **Obverse:** Most of right half of impression. Upper half of seated male figure, facing left to centre of seal, his right hand raised towards body, fore-leg, neck and head of short-horned animal which arches over his head. This presumably tops a *caduceus*, now missing. To his right he holds a long curved object with forked upper end. The sealing appears to be from the same seal as two impressions found in the temple (1600:01 and 1763:09; see Crawford & Matthews 1997, pp. 107 and 111).

## REGISTRATION No. 1853:96

**Dimensions:** 2.15 x 1.55 x 0.72.
**Reverse:** String-impressions.
**Location:** Building 207, Area 272, Square 26. Occupation.
**Description:** Segment of circular sealing of yellowish clay with traces of pink stain. One edge preserved. Obverse very worn, possible *caduceus* visible.

## REGISTRATION No. 1853:97

**Dimensions:** 1.37 x 0.91 x 0.65.
**Reverse:** String-impressions.
**Location:** Building 207, Area 272, Square 26. Occupation.
**Description:** Dark-grey clay, deeply impressed. One edge surviving, with possible wood impressions.
**Obverse:** Schematic human head on left, facing left, and ladder-like motif on right, probably part of one of Kjaerum's gate symbols (1994, p. 342, No. 19). The same impression appears on sealings 1853:96, 99, 100–106 and 109. The drawing is a reconstruction based on all related fragments. The design can be reconstructed as follows: On the left, a standing horned animal with ruffed neck, facing left, with head turned back to centre of seal, and a seated or squatting, nude, human figure who faces left, with one arm raised to the left. His feet rest on a hatched rectangle below him. To its left is a long-legged bird with striped body, facing right; to its right is an animal head, above which are a shield symbol, and a ladder-like motif.

## REGISTRATION No. 1853:98

**Dimensions:** 1.45 x 0.8 x 0.6.
**Reverse:** Possible string-impression.
**Location:** Building 207, Area 272, Square 26. Occupation.
**Description:** Grey clay. **Obverse:** Ladder-like, long, hatched rectangle (8 x 2 squares). See 1853:97 for description of whole scene and list of sealings from same seal.

### REGISTRATION No. 1853:99

**Dimensions:** 2.3 x 1.9 x 0.8.
**Reverse:** Impression of knotted string.
**Location:** Building 207, Area 272, Square 26. Occupation.
**Description:** Grey clay. About half of circular seal impression preserved, including the edge which has finger-prints. **Obverse:** Animal on left with long, ruffed neck, head missing, looking back over its shoulder toward seated, nude figure. Only lower half of body visible, with part of a raised arm. Between the figures is a circular motif, behind the hind-legs of the animal is a hooked motif. See 1853:97 for description of whole scene and list of sealings from same seal.

### REGISTRATION No. 1853:100

**Dimensions:** 2.3 x 1.3 x 1.0.
**Reverse:** Slightly-concave, with parallel string-impressions, possibly from a peg.
**Location:** Building 207, Area 272, Square 26. Occupation.
**Description:** Dark-grey clay. About one quarter of circumference of seal preserved, with finger-prints on edge. **Obverse:** Hatched symbol on right, shield symbol to left.
Bottom left has corner of a hatched square. See 1853:97 for description of whole scene and list of sealings from same seal.

### REGISTRATION No. 1853:101

**Dimensions:** 2.3 x 1.1 x 0.8.
**Reverse:** Deep parallel impressions, one of string.
**Location:** Building 207, Area 272, Square 26. Occupation.
**Description:** Light-grey clay with white inclusions. About one-third of edge of sealing with finger-prints. **Obverse:** Badly worn. Horned animal with ruffed neck, head turned over its shoulder towards centre of seal.
Traces of bird below and to right. See 1853:97 for description of whole scene and list of sealings from same seal.

### REGISTRATION No. 1853:102

**Dimensions:** 1.55 x 0.9 x 0.5.
**Reverse:** One flat surface, one with string.
**Location:** Building 207, Area 272, Square 26. Occupation.
**Description:** Grey clay. Small segment of smooth edge. **Obverse:** Hatched rectangle.
See 1853:97 for description of whole scene and list of sealings from same seal.

### REGISTRATION No. 1853:103

**Dimensions:** 0.9 x 1.4 x 0.4.
**Reverse:** String-impressions.
**Location:** Building 207, Area 272, Square 26. Occupation.
**Description:** Dark-grey, fine clay. Segment of smooth edge with finger-prints. **Obverse:** Animal head on left, with long horns, looking right towards human head. Partly obliterated by thumbprint. See 1853:97 for description of whole scene and list of sealings from same seal.

### REGISTRATION No. 1853:104

**Dimensions:** 1.5 x 1.3 x 1.1.
**Reverse:** Knot-impression.
**Location:** Building 207, Area 272, Square 26. Occupation.
**Description:** Yellowish friable clay. Small segment of smooth edge with two pinholes in it. **Obverse:** Triangular, hatched motif on edge, a shield to its left. See 1853:97 for description of whole scene and list of sealings from same seal.

### REGISTRATION No. 1853:105

**Dimensions:** 0.8 x 1.15 x 0.4.
**Reverse:** Not described.
**Location:** Building 207, Area 272, Square 26. Occupation.
**Description:** Dark-grey clay. Small area of smooth edge preserved. **Obverse:** Long-legged bird facing right. See 1853:97 for description of whole scene and list of sealings from same seal.

## REGISTRATION No. 1853:106

**Dimensions:** 0.6 x 1.2 x 0.75.
**Reverse:** One surface flat, one with possible string-impression.
**Location:** Building 207, Area 272, Square 26. Occupation/ floor.
**Description:** Grey clay. Segment of edge with finger-print. **Obverse:** Part of hatched motif. See 1853:97 for description of whole scene and list of sealings from same seal.

## REGISTRATION No. 1853:107

**Dimensions:** 1.7 x 1.14 x 0.9.
**Reverse:** Deep, smooth indentation, possibly a small peg(?).
**Location:** Building 207, Area 272, Square 26. Occupation.
**Description:** Hard yellowish clay. Approximately one quarter of seal impression. Segment of smooth edge with finger-prints. Design very worn, from bottom right of seal impression. Body, legs and part of neck of animal, facing right, perhaps looking over its shoulder towards centre of seal.

## REGISTRATION No. 1853:108

**Dimensions:** 1.65 x 1.0 x 1.1.
**Reverse:** Part of knot.
**Location:** Building 207 Area 272, Square 26. Occupation.
**Description:** Yellowish clay. Segment of smooth edge. **Obverse:** Part of hatched motif.

## REGISTRATION No. 1853:109

**Dimensions:** 1.0 x 1.8 x 0.5.
**Reverse:** String-impressions.
**Location:** Building 207, Area 272, Square 26. Occupation.
**Description:** Dark-grey clay. About one quarter of smooth edge with finger-prints. Part of lower and lower left edge preserved. **Obverse:** Long-legged bird with striped body, facing right towards hatched square. Traces of human feet above square and of legs of animal above bird's back. See 1853:97 for description of whole scene and list of sealings from same seal.

## REGISTRATION No. 1853:116

**Dimensions:** 1.8 x 1.4 x 0.4.
**Reverse:** One deep indentation, perhaps from a rim.
**Location:** Building 207, Area 272, Square 3. Occupation.
**Description:** Friable yellow clay. **Obverse:** Edge of impression visible, design illegible.

## REGISTRATION No. 1853:131

**Dimensions:** 1.8 x 1.25 x 0.7.
**Reverse:** String-impression.
**Location:** Building 207, Area 272. Occupation.
**Description:** Fine, slightly-pinkish clay. Oval-shaped with smoothed edge. Small hole, diam 0.3, punched from obverse through sealing.

## REGISTRATION No. 1856:01

**Dimensions:** 2.5 x 2.0 x 1.0.
**Reverse:** Deep impressions of twisted string.
**Location:** Building 207, Area 272, Square 7. Post-abandonment sand.
**Description:** Probably bitumen; one edge of sealing preserved. **Obverse:** Nude figure, head missing, facing left and seated on a small, rectangular, hatched stool/seat. He holds a long straw, which leads into a pot at his feet. Similar to 1021:3, 4 and 5.

## REGISTRATION No. 1864:36

**Dimensions:** 1.5 x 2.0 x 1.3.
**Reverse:** Convex and smooth.
**Location:** Building 207, Area 273, Square 31. Occupation.
**Description:** Grey clay. About half of oblong tag with one surface flattened for sealing. String-hole at one end, string apparently much finer than the usual twisted variety. Flat surface shows about one quarter of design, badly worn. Hatched square in a hollow square. Illegible motif to right, possibly horns; traces of second hatched square to left.

## REGISTRATION No. 1864:43

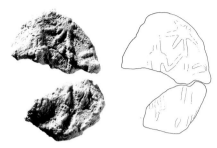

**Dimensions:** (i) 1.0 x 1.7 x 0.5. (ii) 0.95 x 1.5 x 0.5.
**Reverse:** String-impression.
**Location:** Building 207, Area 273, Square 30. Occupation.
**Description:** Two fragments on yellowish clay, possibly from same sealing. (i) Segment of edge with indentation.
**Obverse:** A palm-tree with star-like leaves, to the left of which is upper part of human figure with one arm outstretched to tree. To right of tree is the possible nose of an animal. Perhaps from same seal as 1893:07.
(ii) Segments of edge with indentation. Design shows possible skirt, lower part of tree and animal leg.

## REGISTRATION No. 1869:05

**Dimensions:** 1.55 x 1.45 x 0.55.
**Reverse:** Knot-impression.
**Location:** Building 207, Area 272. Occupation.
**Description:** Sub-oval fragment of light-brown, fine clay. Small area of smoothed edge. **Obverse:** Skirt and legs of figure facing right, with part of a hatched square below. A damaged animal in left field, head and fore-quarters missing.

## REGISTRATION No. 1869:06

**Dimensions:** 1.2 x 0.7 x 0.55.
**Reverse:** String-impressions.
**Location:** Building 207, Area 272. Occupation.
**Description:** Small, sub-oval fragment of fine, light-brown clay with one flat side.

## REGISTRATION No. 1869:07

**Dimensions:** Length 1.0, width 0.9, thickness 0.6.
**Reverse:** String-impression.
**Location:** Building 207, Area 272. Occupation.
**Description:** Small sub-oval fragment of fine, light-brown clay.
**Obverse:** Angled faces, one smooth, the other with partial impression of possible hatched square. Very worn surface.

## REGISTRATION No. 1869:08

Seven fragments.
**Dimensions:** See below.
**Reverse:** (i–vi) String-impressions.
**Location:** Building 207, Area 272. Occupation.
**Description:** Fine, light-brown clay.
(i) Sub-ovoid with convex, obverse surface, sharp angle to concave smooth side. **Dimensions:** 1.75 x 1.2 x 0.77.
(ii) Sub-rectangular possibly with worn seal impression on obverse. **Dimensions:** 1.27 x 0.98 x 0.6.
(iii) Sub-triangular with curved edges, finger-prints on obverse. **Dimensions:** 1.0 x 0.8 x 0.34.
(iv) Sub-triangular with dot on tip, possibly with worn impression on convex obverse. **Dimensions:** 1.0 x 0.95 x 0.43.
(v) Sub-rectangular with very worn finger-prints on obverse. **Dimensions:** 1.1 x 0.75 x 0.4.
(vi) Pointed, triangular, with small smooth, concave, obverse surface. String-impressions on two surfaces. **Dimensions:** 1.0 x 0.57 x 0.4.
(vii) Worn, sub-ovoid lump with no impressions. **Dimensions:** 0.85 x 0.6 x 0.35.

## REGISTRATION No. 1870:06

**Dimensions:** 1.8 x 2.65 x 1.1.
**Reverse:** Tubular impression at right angles to flat surface, small peg(?).
**Location:** Building 207, Area 273. Floor.
**Description:** Dense green clay, slated and cracked, surface eroded.

## REGISTRATION No. 1873:02

**Dimensions:** 2.95 x 1.15 x 0.75.
**Reverse:** One face is worn and crystalline; the two broken edges have string-impressions.
**Location:** Building 207, Area 272. Hearth.
**Description:** One sub-cuboid fragment, with pointed corner, of light-brown clay. Numerous angular clear inclusions, possibly gypsum crystals. **Obverse:** Smooth and sloping down at one end, no visible impressions.

## REGISTRATION No. 1893:06

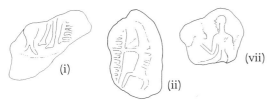

(i)

(ii)

(vii)

**Dimensions:** See below.
**Reverse:** See below.
**Location:** Building 207, Area 272. Midden.
**Description:** Twelve fragments of clay sealings, of fine, grey clay with fragmentary designs on each.
(i) Reverse: String-impression. Part of smoothed edge with finger-print. **Obverse:** Pair of human legs, facing left, with horizontal, hatched motif in right field behind them. Fragment of *caduceus* or table in left field. Linear Style.
**Dimensions:** 1.0 x 2.0 x 1.2.
(ii) Reverse: String-impression. Part of smoothed edge with finger-print. **Obverse:** Part of left margin of seal, inverted scorpion with a hatched, oblong motif to left.
**Dimensions:** 1.6 x 1.1 x 0.8.
(iii) Nothing visible on reverse. Small segment of smoothed edge, with finger-print. **Obverse:** Two parallel linear motifs.
**Dimensions:** 1.6 x 1.2 x 0.8.
(iv) Reverse broken. Fragment of smoothed edge.
**Design:** Several, disjointed, linear motifs including a possible pair of horns.
**Dimensions:** 1.2 x 1.1 x 0.9.
(v) String-mark on reverse, smoothed edge. **Obverse:** Two curved parallel lines on edge of seal.
**Dimensions:** 1.6 x 1.2 x 0.7.
(vi) Possible string-marks on reverse. Small area of smoothed edge with finger-print. **Obverse:** Badly worn. Two raised motifs, parallel to each other.
**Dimensions:** 1.9 x 1.2 x 0.7.
(vii) String-impression on reverse. Small area of smoothed edge. **Obverse:** Very worn, upper half of seated human figure, facing left, with one arm raised to the left towards a hoof. Compare with 1161:04 and related sealings.
**Dimensions:** 1.0 x 1.1 x 0.6.
(viii) String-impression on reverse. Small smoothed area. **Obverse:** Possible hatched motif.
**Dimensions:** 1.2 x 1.1 x 0.5.
(ix) Possible string-impression on reverse.
**Design:** Damaged. Two parallel lines survive.
**Dimensions:** 1.0 x 0.9 x 0.5.
(x) Fragment of smoothed edge with finger-print. String-impression on reverse. Design badly worn. Part of a scorpion and two curved parallel lines, perhaps horns.
**Dimensions:** 0.45 x 1.1 x 0.7.

(xi) Small fragment no edge. **Obverse:** A pair of human legs, facing left. Linear Style.
**Dimensions:** 0.5 x 0.8 x 0.42.
(xii) Small fragment, no edge. **Obverse:** Human torso facing left, badly worn.
**Dimensions:** 0.8 x 0.75 x 0.3.

## REGISTRATION No. 1893:07

**Dimensions:** 2.15 x 1.45 x 1.1.
**Reverse:** Knot-impression.
**Location:** Building 207, Area 272. Midden.
**Description:** Yellowish clay with salty inclusions, badly cracked; part of smoothed edge. **Obverse:** Segment of top and right edge of impression. Head and long horns of animal facing right, head turned over its shoulder, towards palm-tree with star-like leaves. To the left an unidentified motif. From same seal as 1864:43(?).

## REGISTRATION No. 1893:08

**Dimensions:** See below.
**Reverse:** See below.
**Location:** Building 207, Area 272. Midden.
**Description:** Four fragments of clay sealings, all of yellowish clay with white shelly inclusions.
(i) Semicircular. String-marks on reverse. Part of edge. One smooth surface with indentation, but no design visible. **Dimensions:** 2.1 x 1.6 x 0.95.
(ii) Part of right edge of sealing. Possible string-marks on reverse. **Obverse:** Worn figure of animal looking back over its shoulder to centre of seal. **Dimensions:** 1.7 x 1.1 x 0.9.
(iii) Irregular fragment, string-impression on one face. **Obverse:** Badly worn; parallel striations visible.
**Dimensions:** 1.3 x 0.9 x 0.6.
(iv) Small irregular fragment. Traces of design: tree or frond on right, on left a horned animal with head stretched up, with a possible second animal to right of tree.
**Dimensions:** 0.6 x 1.0 x 0.45.

REGISTRATION No. 1893:09
**Dimensions:** 2.5 x 1.4 x 1.0.
**Reverse:** Knot-impression.
**Location:** Building 207, Area 272. Midden.
**Description:** Yellowish clay with salty inclusions. Left edge, and about one third of large circular seal. Segment of smoothed edge. **Obverse:** Lower part of standing figure in tiered skirt, facing left, vertical line on either side of figure, perhaps a spear and shield.

REGISTRATION No. 2057:09

**Dimensions:** 2.1 x 1.7 x 1.0.
**Reverse:** String-impression.
**Location:** Building 56, Area 93. Floor.
**Description:** Yellow-green clay, smoothed edge. Design distorted by pressure into oval. **Obverse:** Standing nude figure looking to his left, hand outstretched towards a horned animal head. Below the animal's head is a small bush or frond. Finely cut, but badly worn (possibly Style Ib).

REGISTRATION No. 2123:01

**Dimensions:** 1.7 x 1.4 x 0.6.
**Reverse:** String-impression.
**Location:** Building 56, Area 77. Occupation.
**Description:** Fragment of grey clay. Area of concave edge has finger-prints. **Obverse:** Highly-stylised, linear figure on the left, arm held up to the right. A possible second-such figure is in the centre of the seal, with a diagonal line above it. Linear Style. Estimated diam. of seal 1.5.

REGISTRATION No. 2141:01

**Dimensions:** 1.5 x 1.7 x 0.5.
**Reverse:** Worn; possible string-impression.
**Location:** Building 56, Area 68. Occupation.
**Description:** Fine, pinkish clay. **Obverse:** Most of impression present. In the centre a rosette framed by a square, a six-pointed star below the square, and a standing horned animal on either side of it. The animals face outwards, but look back over their shoulders towards each other. Above the horns of one is an unidentified motif. The use of the point drill suggests this sealing may belong to Kjaerum's Style Ib/II.

REGISTRATION No. 2143:01
**Dimensions:** 1.6 x 1.0 x 1.3.
**Reverse:** Surface missing.
**Location:** Building 55, Area 81. Occupation.
**Description:** Orange clay. Possibly burnt.
**Obverse:** Fragmentary seal impression, showing a rectangle with horizontal lines across it.

REGISTRATION No. 2149:02
**Dimensions:** 1.7 x 0.9 x 0.7.
**Reverse:** Surface missing.
**Location:** Building 55, Area 80. Make-up.
**Description:** Yellow clay.
**Obverse:** Three parallel incised lines.

REGISTRATION No. 2157:05

**Dimensions:** 1.6 x 1.3 x 0.6.
**Reverse:** Knot-impression.
**Location:** Building 56, Area 68. Make-up.
**Description:** Yellow clay. Possible string-hole on right side.
**Obverse:** Tiered skirts of three standing figures facing left.

## REGISTRATION NO. 2171:02

**Dimensions:** 1.6 x 1.0 x 0.7.
**Reverse:** String-impressions.
**Location:** Building 57, Area 74. Make-up.
**Description:** Burnt brown clay. One area of smoothed edge, part of which has been flattened. Obverse (from left to right): a tree or frond; a standing, nude, male figure, facing right and holding a standard. The standard is topped by a crescent on its back, with a rosette or sun above.
A second, damaged figure faces left on the other side of the standard. The style is linear and deeply incised. Kjaerum's Style Ib. See 5176:07 for another Style Ib sealing. Estimated diam. of seal 1.1.

## REGISTRATION NO. 2570:11

**Dimensions:** Max. length 3.2, max. width 2.2.
**Reverse:** Bifacial.
**Location:** Building 50, Area 57. Floor.
**Description:** Approximately oval tag of burnt orange clay. Break at one end, where string pulled away. Finger-prints on each face. One seal impression on each side.
Side 1: Heavily burnt. Central hatched rectangle (2 x 4 squares). A pole extends from the top corner of the rectangle, to the right, to rest on the shoulders of a standing figure in a short skirt, facing left, arms up to either side, touching the rectangle. There is a second, badly-damaged figure to the left of the central rectangle. Illegible motif above rectangle on edge of seal. Side 2: Design distorted by pressure. A wheel of four-horned animals, necks joined by a large, hatched circle. One animal faces right, and its neighbour left. The rest are destroyed. Between the heads are other motifs: a standing man, and part of a circle with loops on the outer edge. These seem to be repeated in opposing quadrants.

## REGISTRATION NO. 3040: 01

**Dimensions:** (i) 2.52 x 1.8 x 0.85. (ii) 1.73 x 1.1 x 0.65.
**Reverse:** Flat surface with possible plaster inclusions.
**Location:** Building 302, Area 408. Sand.
**Description:** Half of a blank sealing(?). Two pieces, originally joined, with smoothed edge and indentations on obverse. No identifiable motifs.

## REGISTRATION NO. 3041:16

**Dimensions:** (i) 2.15 x 1.5 x 1.05. (ii) 1.85 x 1.32 x 0.82. (iii) 1.95 x 1.1 x 0.72. (iv) 2.0 x 0.78 x 0.45.
Plus twelve smaller pieces.
**Reverse:** (i) n/a. (ii) Tubular impression tapering to a point, perhaps made by a small peg. (iii) Parallel striations. (iv) One flat surface with parallel striations.
Location: Building 301, Area 409. Collapse.
**Description:** Sixteen fragments of greenish-yellow clay with some white, crystalline inclusions. Possibly sealings.
(i) Pinched, roughly triangular fragment.
(ii) Irregular fragment. (iii) One smooth edge, one smooth surface. (iv) One smooth surface.

## REGISTRATION NO. 3041:18

**Dimensions:** (i) 2.6 x 2.05 x 0.9, estimated diam. of seal 1.2. (ii) 1.8 x 1.3 x 0.88.
**Reverse:** (i) Knot-impression and two parallel ridges. (ii) Uneven smoothed area.
**Location:** Building 301, Area 409, Collapse.
**Description:** (i) Fine, grey clay. One arc of smoothed edge. Seated human figure looking left. His right hand touches the rump of a (damaged) inverted, horned animal with head to the left. Below the figure to the right is another horned animal facing right, hind-legs missing. Above its rump is a possible crab with a St Andrew's cross on its shell.

## REGISTRATION No. 3041:21

**Dimensions:** 1.4 x 1.1 x 0.45.
**Reverse:** Knot-impression.
**Location:** Building 301, Area 409. Collapse.
**Description:** Roughly rectangular piece of fine, grey clay with two smoothed edges. Small arc of circular sealing preserved. To the left are a fore-leg with hoof and the rear hoof of an animal, drawn together. To the right are three perpendicular motifs parallel to each other.

## REGISTRATION No. 3041:26

**Dimensions:** 3.13 x 2.95 x 1.65.
**Reverse:** Worn impressions of string and knot.
**Location:** Building 201, Area 409. Collapse.
**Description:** Very powdery, brown clay with white inclusions. Deep edge, slightly corrugated.
**Obverse:** Badly damaged, a pair of lines forming a right angle with a possible second pair inside them.

## REGISTRATION No. 3503:05

**Dimensions:** 3.4 x 2.8 x 1.4, estimated diam. of seal 1.8.
**Reverse:** Convex, smooth.
**Location:** Building 300, Area 400. Occupation.
**Description:** Lentoid tag of fine, grey clay with white inclusions, originally with string through long axis. One end now broken away, apparently from around knot. Upper surface smoothed. Badly-worn circular impression partly visible. Motifs include a horned animal perhaps with its head turned back over its shoulder, and to its right the lower part of a human figure with a long skirt, facing left. Between the figures is a possible jar.

## REGISTRATION No. 3503:8

**Dimensions:** 2.63 x 1.91 x 1.16.
**Reverse:** Surface missing.
**Location:** Building 300, Area 400. Occupation.
**Description:** Possible sealing fragment. Sub-rectangular piece of light-grey/green clay with tiny white flecks, one surface carefully smoothed.

## REGISTRATION No. 3515:11

**Dimensions:** 1.6 x 1.18.
**Reverse:** Damaged.
**Location:** Building 300, Area 401. Make-up.
**Description:** Small fragment of fine clay with one stone chip as inclusion. **Obverse:** To the right the hind-legs of a standing animal; to the left the skirt and feet of a human figure facing left. From a well-cut seal.

## REGISTRATION No. 4028:21

**Dimensions:** 1.2 x 0.97 x 0.5.
**Reverse:** Worn.
**Location:** Building 205, Area 235. Floor.
**Description:** Fine, yellowish clay. Part of edge extant. **Obverse:** Vertical hatched motif, perhaps a shield, with a possible fragmentary human head to the right. Perhaps from same seal as 5155:06.

## REGISTRATION No. 4041:06

**Dimensions:** 2.12 x 1.25 x 1.03.
**Reverse:** One deep string-impression.
**Location:** Building 208, Area 238. Occupation.
**Description:** Light-grey clay. Left lower quarter of sealing preserved, with clear finger-prints. **Obverse:** Body and legs of a standing male animal facing right, head and neck missing, but curved tips of horns visible above.

## REGISTRATION No. 4088:09

**Dimensions:** 1.6 x 1.3 x 0.8.
**Reverse:** Irregular, with possible string-impression.
**Location:** Building 205, Area 237. Occupation.
**Description:** Cubic fragment of light-brown clay with a large stony inclusion (0.7 x 0.4) and one side burnt to a dark-grey. **Obverse:** Two sides of a squared, smoothed surface, later burnt to a dark-grey. Smaller extant surface has finger-print impressions.

## REGISTRATION No. 4096:05

**Dimensions:** 2.5 x 1.6 x 0.8.
**Reverse:** Two parallel string-impressions.
**Location:** Building 205, Area 237. Occupation.
**Description:** Possible jar sealing. Sub-ovoid lump of light-brown, fine clay. Surface partly baked to orange.
**Obverse:** Smoothed edges appear to have been pushed by a finger; edges covered with finger-prints.

## REGISTRATION No. 4104:07

**Dimensions:** (i) 0.8 x 0.7 x 0.6. (ii) 0.65 x 0.45 x 0.4.
**Reverse:** Surface missing.
**Location:** Building 205, Area 237. Occupation.
**Description:** Two possible fragments of burnt clay. Now very dark-grey. (i) Sub-ovoid/angular with possible impressions or heat warping. (ii) Sub-ovoid.

## REGISTRATION No. 4197:01

**Dimensions:** 3.3 x 2.4 x 1.05.
**Reverse:** Knot-impression.
**Location:** Building 209, Area 247. Floor.
**Description:** Pale-grey clay with white inclusions. Central part of a large seal impression; minimum estimated diam. of seal 2.2. **Obverse:** Kneeling, male, horned quadruped, possibly a bull, facing left. Above him a smaller, standing quadruped, facing left, looking back over its shoulder. To the upper right is the raised arm of a standing human figure, to the left, unidentified motifs.

## REGISTRATION No. 5016:02

**Dimensions:** 3.2 x 2.2 x 0.8.
**Reverse:** Smooth.
**Location:** Building 221, Area 301. Collapse.
**Description:** Lozenge-shaped tag, originally squeezed round a thread. Holes for thread remain at each end. Fine, light-grey clay. Impression of rectangular or cylindrical seals, badly distorted and worn. (Possibly two partly-superimposed sealings.) On the left is a hatched square, then a human figure and an animal.

## REGISTRATION No. 5056:21

**Dimensions:** 1.7 x 1.8 x 0.85.
**Reverse:** String-impression.
**Location:** Building 222, Area 304. Floor.
**Description:** Fine, light-grey clay, one smoothed edge, possible string-hole. **Obverse:** Traces of sealing on one face, showing sun symbol and possible animal head.

## REGISTRATION No. 5065:01

**Dimensions:** 2.3 x 2.0 x 0.9.
**Reverse:** Three parallel string-impressions.
**Location:** Building 222, Area 305. Floor.
**Description:** Jar sealing. Sandy, light-grey clay. Edge smooth.
**Obverse:** Virtually-complete seal impression, distorted by squeezing. **Design:** Standard with crescent on top, above a hatched square. To left is a rampant, horned, male animal. Second, damaged, rampant animal to right. Goose or duck in left field, looking over its shoulder to the left.

## REGISTRATION No. 5099:10

Three clay fragments, possibly used for sealing, located adjacent to cooking pot 5099:08. No further description.

## REGISTRATION No. 5099:16

**Dimensions:** 4.2 x 2.5 x 0.9 (largest fragment).
**Reverse:** Surface missing.
**Location:** Building 220, Area 309. Sand.
**Description:** Six fragments of hardened, pale-grey clay. No impressions clearly visible.

## REGISTRATION No. 5110:01

 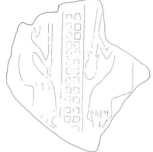

**Dimensions:** 2.5 x 2.4 x 1.1.
**Reverse:** Knot and string-impressions.
**Location:** Building 220, Area 310. Floor.
**Description:** Hard pink clay. Approximately circular sealing with two segments missing. Almost half of the circumference of the seal is preserved; part of the edge is smooth, the rest broken away. **Obverse:** Long, hatched rectangle (2 x 11 squares) in the centre of the design. On either side are seated human figures in long hatched skirts, facing inwards, bent arms raised upwards. Figure on right holds a straw leading into a jar at waist height. Left-hand figure also raises one arm. Possibly from the same seal as 5143:01.

## REGISTRATION No. 5111:02

**Dimensions:** 2.0 x 2.0 x 1.0.
**Reverse:** Knot-impression.
**Location:** Building 220, Area 310. Floor.
**Description:** Bitumen, or bitumen and clay, with white inclusions. Irregular shape.
**Obverse:** Apparently the central portion of a large design. In the centre is a standing, bearded figure in a long tiered skirt, facing left, arms extended to either side. To the right he touches the neck of a very fragmentary animal with its head turned back over its shoulder, while to the left he holds a stick or spear-shaft. Traces of a second figure to the left of spear, also holding it. Possibly from the same seal as 5137:01 and 02.

## REGISTRATION No. 5133:01

**Dimensions:** 1.4 x 1.3 x 0.65.
**Reverse:** Deep peg-shaped indentation.
**Location:** Building 220, Area 310. Feature.
**Description:** Dark-grey clay. Fragment of original edge with finger-print. **Obverse:** Design divided into four fields by cross formed by four hatched rectangles. Where the arms of the cross meet, the resulting square is un-hatched. Triangular or bow-shaped motif in two surviving quadrants. From same seal as 5143:15 and 5153:01.

## REGISTRATION No. 5136:01

**Dimensions:** 2.3 x 2.0 x 1.8.
**Reverse:** Knot-impression.
**Location:** Building 220, Area 311. Collapse.
**Description:** Burnt black clay. Virtually-complete, circular impression preserved; two opposing edges broken off.
Estimated diam. of seal 2.0. **Obverse:** Badly worn. Part of a standing, skirted, human figure on the left, and a fringed square to the right. Five other sealings from same seal: see 5143:02.

## REGISTRATION No. 5136:02

**Dimensions:** 2.2 x 1.8 x 1.0.
**Reverse:** Surface missing.
**Location:** Building 220, Area 220. Collapse.
**Description:** Friable, dark-grey clay. About one quarter of impression present; badly worn. Two motifs, one a rosette or star, the other illegible.

## REGISTRATION No. 5136:06

**Dimensions:** 2.6 x 1.8 x 1.1.
**Reverse:** Smooth and Slightly-convex.
**Location:** Building 220, Area 311. Collapse.
**Description:** Hard, greenish clay, forming segment of ovoid bulla with string-hole visible in section. A thin additional skin of fine clay has been added to take the impression.

**Obverse:** A pair of feet, turned to the left, below them and to the right a horizontal 'foot' motif, below this again is the head and neck of a short-horned animal looking left. A drilled motif, possibly an animal body, to the right of the damaged legs.

## REGISTRATION NO. 5136:11

**Dimensions:** (i) 1.7 x 1.4 x 0.4. (ii) 1.3 x 1.1 x 0.3.
**Reverse:** Flat and smooth, with impression of a slightly-raised edge.
**Location:** Building 220, Area 311. Collapse.
**Description:** Two joining fragments of pale-grey clay. Worn and distorted. (i) Standing figure in tiered skirt, facing left. To left, fragmentary monkey-like figure, facing left, apparently kneeling, with a long tail. Fragmentary device to lower right of standing figure. (ii) Head and torso of standing figure.

## REGISTRATION NO. 5137:01

**Dimensions:** 2.5 x 2.5 x 1.0.
**Reverse:** Multiple string-impressions.
**Location:** Building 220, Area 310. Floor.
**Description:** White gritty clay. Part of lower edge preserved. Central portion of design from large seal.
**Obverse:** A standing male figure with a long tiered skirt, head turned to the left. His arms are stretched out on either side. To the left he holds a spear/stick with forked ends, which is held on the other side by a squatting, monkey-like figure which faces him. To the right he touches a second figure. From same seal as 5111:02 and 5137:02. Drawing is a reconstruction based on all related fragments.

## REGISTRATION NO. 5137:02

**Dimensions:** 2.1 x 1.3 x 1.9.
**Reverse:** String-impression.
**Location:** Building 220, Area 310. Floor.
**Description:** Black, burnt clay. Finger-print on left edge. Bottom left quarter of seal. **Obverse:** On left is a seated naked figure, holding a vertical spear or stick to the right. To the right of this is a standing figure (damaged), facing left, in a long, striated skirt, also with one hand grasping the stick. From same seal as 5111:02 and 5137:01.

## REGISTRATION NO. 5138:05

**Dimensions:** 1.6 x 1.1 x 0.9.
**Reverse:** String-impression.
**Location:** Building 220, Area 312. Floor.
**Description:** Dark-grey clay. Part of edge preserved with finger-prints. Segment of right half of impression. Head and neck of a long-horned animal facing left. Two parallel lines to left of head.

## REGISTRATION NO. 5138:07

**Dimensions:** 1.9 x 1.8 x 1.1.
**Reverse:** Knot-impression.
**Location:** Building 220, Area 312. Floor.
**Description:** Sandy, buff clay. Part of smoothed edge with finger-prints. **Obverse:** Torso of human figure, possibly wearing a hatched skirt, grasping a horned animal to the right. The animal is vertical and facing left, looking back over its shoulder. Illegible motif in right field.

## REGISTRATION NO. 5138:08

**Dimensions:** 1.0 x 0.9 x 0.6.
**Reverse:** Worn.
**Location:** Building 220, Area 312. Floor.
**Description:** Buff clay. Very worn, but edge of seal and traces of sealing apparent on one side.
**Obverse:** The head of a long-horned animal facing left.

## REGISTRATION No. 5143:01

**Dimensions:** 2.0 x 1.8 x 0.9.
**Reverse:** Possible string-impressions.
**Location:** Building 220, Area 311. Floor.
**Description:** Pale-yellowish clay. The top left edge is preserved and has finger-prints on it. **Obverse:** Top left quadrant of design. Vertical, hatched rectangle in centre (2 x 6 squares extant) with vertical line to left, perhaps the frame of a loom. To the left is the torso of a human figure, facing right one arm raised towards the loom. To the right is the arm of a second figure, also raised towards loom. Possibly from the same seal as 5111:01.

## REGISTRATION No. 5143:02

**Dimensions:** 2.7 x 2.4 x 1.1.
**Reverse:** Knot-impression.
**Location:** Building 220, Area 311. Floor.
**Description:** Pinky grey clay. Virtually-complete circular impression, distorted and worn. Lower and right edge preserved. **Obverse:** Two round holes through which a string seems to have been threaded. Two standing figures, the one on the left in a striated skirt, that on the right in a tiered skirt, touching a fringed square, the centre of which is obscured by damage to the surface. The following sealings appear to be impressed with the same seal: 5136:01, 5143:03, 5143:06, 5143:08, 5143:14. The drawing is a reconstruction based on all related fragments. The complete design can be reconstructed as follows: Two standing human figures in long skirts. The left-hand figure has arms raised to either side and faces left, the right-hand one holds his arms downwards and also faces left. Both touch, or carry, a square between them, perhaps a podium, which has a damaged raised area in the centre. Above the square is a crescent, the horns of which enclose a deeply cut star with rays; a second similar star below the square.

## REGISTRATION No. 5143:03

**Dimensions:** (i) 1.7 x 1.0 x 0.6. (ii) 2.0 x 2.1 x 1.7.
**Reverse:** Two horizontal string-impressions on large fragment.
**Location:** Building 220, Area 311. Floor.
**Description:** Greenish grey clay with white inclusions.

(i) Irregular, featureless fragment. (ii) Three-quarters of circular impression; lower right edge missing, part of top edge preserved. Obverse: Two standing figures in long, hatched skirts, the left-hand figure with arms raised to either side. The right-hand figure has arms held downwards. Both touch a rectangular, fringed square with concave top between them, perhaps a podium. It is partly obscured by a raised lump, probably a damaged area of the seal. Above the square is a crescent, the horns of which enclose a star. Estimated diam. of seal 2.1. Five other sealings from same seal: see 5143:02.

## REGISTRATION No. 5143:06

**Dimensions:** 2.2 x 1.8 x 1.4.
**Reverse:** String-impressions and some parallel striations.
**Location:** Building 220, Area 311. Floor.
**Description:** Hard, pink, baked clay. Design incomplete and damaged; part of lower and right edges preserved.
**Obverse:** Standing figure in a tiered skirt, feet to the left, head missing, arms extended by his sides. Traces of a square to the left. Five other sealings from same seal: see 5143:02.

## REGISTRATION No. 5143:08

**Dimensions:** 2.1 x 2.1 x 1.1.
**Reverse:** Knot-impression.
**Location:** Building 220, Area 311. Floor.
**Description:** Pinkish clay. Sub-circular piece; part of right-hand edge preserved, with finger-prints.

**Obverse:** Part of two standing figures in long hatched skirts. The right-hand figure is standing with arms extended by his sides. His (largely missing) head is turned to the left. The left-hand figure has only part of the skirt preserved, and an arm held up to the right. Between the figures is a fringed square, which both are touching, largely obscured by a lump representing damaged area of seal. Five other sealings from same seal: see 5143:02.

### REGISTRATION No. 5143:09

**Dimensions:** 1.8 x 1.8 x 0.5.
**Reverse:** Two parallel striations.
**Location:** Building 220, Area 311. Floor.
**Description:** Fine, pale-grey clay. One edge is smooth.
**Obverse:** Part of at least four concentric circles. Touching the edge of the seal above the circles is part of a crescent containing a star and, to the right, part of a hatched square. Linear Style.

### REGISTRATION No. 5143:10

**Dimensions:** 1.4 x 1.1 x 0.8.
**Reverse:** Possible string-impression.
**Location:** Building 220, Area 311. Floor.
**Description:** Buff, gritty clay. Edges broken off. Top right quarter of impression. **Obverse:** Head of long-horned animal facing left. Behind the neck is part of a curved line.

### REGISTRATION No. 5143:14

**Dimensions:** 2.3 x 2.4 x 1.1.
**Reverse:** Multiple string-impressions.
**Location:** Building 220, Area 311. Floor.
**Description:** Pinky, gritty clay. About two-thirds preserved, including part of lower edge, with finger-prints.

**Obverse:** Standing, bearded figure on the right, wearing a long, hatched skirt and facing left. To the left, he touches a square, possibly a podium, with clumsy round lump in the middle, probably a damaged area of the seal. Above the square is a crescent, its horns enclosing a star. Left of the podium are traces of second standing figure. Five other sealings from same seal: see 5143:02.

### REGISTRATION No. 5143:15

**Dimensions:** 2.2 x 1.9 x 1.1.
**Reverse:** Two deep, parallel, string-marks.
**Location:** Building 220, Area 311. Floor.
**Description:** Burnt, black clay, with white inclusions, badly cracked. About half of edge preserved, with finger-prints.
**Obverse:** Two-thirds of an impression. The design is divided into four fields by a cross. Arms of cross formed by rectangle filled by striations. Where the arms of the cross meet, the resulting square is undecorated. A triangle is visible in each of the upper fields. Estimated diam. of seal 1.8. From same seal as 5133:01 and 5153:01. Drawing is a composite.

### REGISTRATION No. 5147:02

**Dimensions:** 2.6 x 1.3 x 0.9.
**Reverse:** Possible string-impression, and deep tubular hole, diam. c.0.5.
**Location:** Building 220, Area 310. Floor.
**Description:** Burnt grey clay. The top left edge is preserved; finger-prints. **Obverse:** Very worn seal impression, showing torso of figure with head turned to the right, and arm outstretched to the left, holding an animal, which faces left, and looks back towards the central figure. To the right, unidentified motif.

## REGISTRATION No. 5153:01

**Dimensions:** 1.7 x 1.3 x 0.8.
**Reverse:** Deep tubular impression, diam. c.0.4.
**Location:** Building 220, Area 311. Floor.
**Description:** Burnt grey clay. Central part of impression, no edge preserved.
**Obverse:** Cross with striated arms and undecorated central area. Two triangles visible in angles of the arms. From the same seal as 5143:15 and 5133:01.

## REGISTRATION No. 5155:06

**Dimensions:** 1.6 x 3.0 x 0.9.
**Reverse:** Knot-impression.
**Location:** Building 220, Area 310. Floor.
**Description:** Light-grey clay, two pieces joined. Two-thirds of lower part of circular sealing. Smoothed edges. **Obverse:** A standing nude figure (head missing) facing left and holding to the right an oblong, horizontally hatched motif, incomplete, probably a shield. To left of this is damaged figure of standing horned animal facing left with head thrown back.
Estimated diam. of seal 2.3. Possibly from the same seal as 4028:21.

## REGISTRATION No. 5155:07

**Dimensions:** 2.0 x 2.4 x 1.0.
**Reverse:** Two parallel string-impressions.
**Location:** Building 220, Area 310. Floor.
**Description:** Fine, grey clay. About one quarter of impression preserved. Part of smoothed edge with finger-prints. **Obverse:** Left edge of seal, with seated human figure facing right, one arm outstretched towards a broken motif, perhaps an animal.

## REGISTRATION No. 5155:08

**Dimensions:** 0.9 x 1.0 x 0.5.
**Reverse:** Surface destroyed.
**Location:** Building 220, Area 310. Floor.
**Description:** Fragment of grey clay. Segment of smoothed edge. **Obverse:** Two converging lines, possibly horns.

## REGISTRATION No. 5167:02

**Dimensions:** 1.9 x 0.1 x 0.9.
**Reverse:** Knot-impression.
**Location:** Building 220, Area 310. Floor.
**Description:** Light-yellowish clay. Half of circular sealing, perhaps with part of design pinched off. Section of smoothed left and right edges. **Obverse:** Seated figure with unusual square shoulders, facing right. Behind him, to the left, is a notched, curved object.

## REGISTRATION No. 5167:03

**Dimensions:** 1.5 x 1.7 x 0.9.
**Reverse:** String-impression.
**Location:** Building 220, Area 310. Floor.
**Description:** Hard, pinkish clay. One straight, smooth edge. One quadrant of impression survives. **Obverse:** Three unidentifiable linear motifs, roughly parallel to each other.

## REGISTRATION No. 5167:20

**Dimensions:** 0.75 x 0.85 x 1.4.
**Reverse:** String-impression.
**Location:** Building 220, Area 310. Floor.
**Description:** Very dark grey clay with white inclusions. Pinched edge with deep hollows, probably finger impressions. Lower left segment of design. **Obverse:** Lower legs of standing human, facing left. Unidentified motif to right.

## REGISTRATION No. 5168:04

**Dimensions:** 1.5 x 1.2 x 0.7.
**Reverse:** String-impression.
**Location:** Building 220,
Area 309. Occupation.
**Description:** Fine, grey clay.
Part of edge extant, with finger-prints.
**Obverse:** Part of hatched rectangle.

## REGISTRATION No. 5176:03

**Dimensions:** 2.0 x 2.05 x 1.9.
**Reverse:** String-impression and one flat surface.
**Location:** Building 220, Area 309. Floor.
**Description:** Light-grey clay. About one quarter of design extant. Poor condition. **Obverse:** Badly damaged quadruped facing right, to the left and at right angles to it is a standing, skirted, human figure, one arm raised towards the animal.

## REGISTRATION No. 5176:04

**Dimensions:** 0.95 x 0.72 x 0.5.
**Reverse:** No impression.
**Location:** Building 220, Area 309. Floor.
**Description:** Light-grey, fine clay. One small area of smooth edge. **Obverse:** Crescent with star above. Possibly from same seal as 5176:14.

## REGISTRATION No. 5176:06

**Dimensions:** 1.5 x 1.2 x 0.6.
**Reverse:** String-impression.
**Location:** Building 220, Area 309. Floor.
**Description:** Light-grey clay. Segment of smoothed edge. Trace of edge of seal impression, design illegible.

## REGISTRATION No. 5176:07

**Dimensions:** 1.8 x 2.0 x 1.0.
**Reverse:** Knot-impression.
**Location:** Building 220, Area 309. Floor.
**Description:** Fine, light-grey clay. Two-thirds of the impression of a small seal. Estimated diam. of seal 1.85. Smoothed edge with finger-impression and indentation.
**Obverse:** Two monkey-like figures holding a central, crescent-topped standard, with a star above. Unidentified motif behind monkey to the left. Kjaerum's Style Ib(?). For another Style Ib seal see 2171:02.

## REGISTRATION No. 5176:08

**Dimensions:** 1.1 x 1.65 x 0.9.
**Reverse:** String-impressions.
**Location:** Building 220, Area 309. Floor.
**Description:** Fine, light-grey clay. Area of smoothed edge.
**Obverse:** To the left, top of palm-frond; to the right an animal head with short horns, facing the frond. Left of the frond, part of a second animal head, also facing it. Perhaps from same seal as 5176:10.

## REGISTRATION No. 5176:09

**Dimensions:** 0.95 x 0.9 x 0.8.
**Reverse:** Not recorded.
**Location:** Building 220, Area 309. Floor.
**Description:** Fine, grey clay. Small fragment, edge of seal visible. **Obverse:** Part of a possible hatched triangle.

## REGISTRATION No. 5176:10

**Dimensions:** 1.7 x 1.6 x 0.8.
**Reverse:** Knot-impression.
**Location:** Building 220, Area 309. Floor.
**Description:** Light-grey clay with white inclusions.
**Obverse:** Central portion survives. Two horizontal rows of hatched squares, deeply impressed. Neck and head of animal with short horns protruding from it on right, facing towards palm-frond. Neck of second animal to left of frond. Perhaps from same seal 5176:08.

## REGISTRATION No. 5176:11

**Dimensions:** 1.85 x 0.85 x 0.75.
**Reverse:** Smooth, convex surface with fine, parallel lines.
**Location:** Building 220, Area 309. Floor.
**Description:** Hard buff clay. Possibly part of tag or label. Smoothed edge with finger-prints. **Obverse:** Segment of edge of seal. Human head and top of spear. See 1161:04 for reconstruction of whole design and list of other sealings from same seal.

## REGISTRATION No. 5176:12

**Dimensions:** 1.4 x 1.15 x 0.7.
**Reverse:** String-impression.
**Location:** Building 220, Area 309. Floor.
**Description:** Hard, light-grey clay. Segment of smoothed edge with finger-print. **Obverse:** Design from right edge of impression: upper part of figure of stick-like human, with raised arms. Linear Style. Probably from same seal as 5176:13.

## REGISTRATION No. 5176:13

**Dimensions:** 1.1 x 1.4 x 1.05.
**Reverse:** String-impressions.
**Location:** Building 220, Area 309. Floor.
**Description:** Fine, grey clay. Small area of smoothed edge with finger-print.
**Obverse:** Lower right segment. Lower half of human figure with one leg raised. Probably from same seal as 5176:12.

## REGISTRATION No. 5176:14

**Dimensions:** 1.1 x 1.0 x 0.6.
**Reverse:** Slightly concave.
**Location:** Building 220, Area 309. Floor.
**Description:** Dark-grey, fine clay. Raised edge of seal impression visible. **Obverse:** Horizontal crescent with star or sun in the curve, and to the right the damaged head, shoulder and arm of a human figure. Deeply cut. Possibly from the same seal as 5176:04.

## REGISTRATION No. 5176:15

**Dimensions:** 1.4 x 1.0 x 1.1.
**Reverse:** String-impressions.
**Location:** Building 220, Area 309. Floor.
**Description:** Light-grey clay. Slightly-concave, smoothed edge with finger-print.

## REGISTRATION No. 5178:01

**Dimensions:** 1.45 x 1.2 x 0.5.
**Reverse:** String-impression.
**Location:** Building 220, Area 309. Make-up.
**Description:** Fine, sandy clay. One smoothed edge, with finger-prints.
**Obverse:** Schematic human head and shoulders facing right, one arm raised to right, touching vertical line.

## REGISTRATION No. 5210:06

**Dimensions:** 2.85 x 1.75 x 1.2.
**Reverse:** Surface missing.
**Location:** Building 220, Area 314. Occupation.
**Description:** Two fragments of fine, unbaked, grey clay. Sub-oval. Segment of disk with string-impression running through it. Upper and lower surfaces smooth. No impression.

## REGISTRATION No. 5211:16

**Dimensions:** 2.2 x 1.4 x 0.63.
**Reverse:** Knot-impression.
**Location:** Building 220, Area 314. Occupation.
**Description:** Unbaked greenish clay, with numerous, tiny, white inclusions. Left edge, and part of lower edge of seal impression preserved. **Obverse:** Badly worn. Possible seated, naked, human figure, head missing, facing left, one arm raised to the left, holding a curved stick or straw. Estimated diam. of seal 1.65.

## REGISTRATION No. 5500:08

**Dimensions:** 1.8 x 1.2 x 0.74.
**Reverse:** Knot/string-impression.
**Location:** Building 224, Area 316. Sand above building.
**Description:** Dark-grey clay with large, white inclusions. Rectangular fragment, the preserved portion representing the centre and left edge of an impression. **Obverse:** In the centre, the lower part of a standing human figure in long tiered skirt, feet missing, touching a pair of right-angled lines, possibly the legs of a seated figure facing right. Very damaged figure in left field.

## REGISTRATION No. 5500:09

**Dimensions:** 2.5 x 2.15 x 1.15.
**Reverse:** Surface missing.
**Location:** Building 224, Area 316. Sand above building.
**Description:** Coarse, dark-grey clay, with numerous, small, white inclusions. Perhaps fragment of ovoid bulla. String-hole, diam. 0.04, at narrow ends, and impression of string through body of bulla. Further impressions on transverse section, perhaps of a knot.

## REGISTRATION No. 5510:18

**Dimensions:** 1.83 x 1.2 x 0.74.
**Reverse:** One deep string-impression.
**Location:** Building 224, Area 316. Floor.
**Description:** Unbaked fragment of fine, pale-grey clay. One smoothed edge. **Obverse:** About one-third of seal, showing left edge. Standing figure with tiered skirt facing right, one arm raised to right, perhaps holding hand of fragmentary second figure to right. Only part of his tiered skirt is preserved. Between the two figures is a jar. Impressions 1596:2 and 3, from the temple, are from the same seal (Crawford & Matthews 1997, p. 56, Figs. 14 and 15). 5510:31 and 44 are very similar, and may also be from the same seal. 5510:26 is also similar, but not from the same seal.

## REGISTRATION No. 5510:23

**Dimensions:** 1.83 x 1.2 x 0.74.
**Reverse:** Knot-impression.
**Location:** Building 224, Area 316. Floor.
**Description:** Light-grey, unbaked, small fragment of smooth edge of sealing with very small area of impression. **Obverse:** Small arc of edge of impression, with pair of human feet facing left. Part of same sealing as 5510:36.

## REGISTRATION No. 5510:24

Eight fragments.
**Dimensions:** 1.12 x 0.83 x 0.62 (largest fragment).
**Reverse:** Surface missing.

**Location:** Building 224, Area 316. Floor.
**Description:** Eight small pieces of light-grey, unbaked clay, of irregular shapes, with no distinguishing features. 5510:25, 38, 40, 41, 42, 43, 51 amalgamated with 5510:24.

REGISTRATION No. 5510:25
See 5510:24.

REGISTRATION No. 5510:26

**Dimensions:** 1.5 x 0.86 x 0.86.
**Reverse:** Deep, semicircular string-impression and part of another.
**Location:** Building 224, Area 316. Floor.
**Description:** Sub-rectangular fragment of fine, pale-grey clay. One smoothed edge. **Obverse:** Right third of design. Standing figure in tiered skirt on right, head and shoulders missing. To left, fragmentary remains of second figure in similar skirt. Similar to 5510: 18 (q.v.) and related sealings, but not from the same seal.

REGISTRATION No. 5510:27
**Dimensions:** 2.25 x 1.9 x 1.33.
**Reverse:** Surface missing.
**Location:** Building 224, Area 316. Floor.
**Description:** Possible sealing. Unbaked, light-greenish lump, of irregular shape, with four lines on one surface.

REGISTRATION No. 5510:28

**Dimensions:** 2.56 x 1.26 x 0.95.
**Reverse:** One smooth surface.
**Location:** Building 224, Area 316. Floor.

**Description:** Light-grey, unbaked, sub-triangular fragment; segment of smoothed edge with triangular indentation. Poor condition, cracked down centre. **Obverse:** Central part of design. On left, hind-quarters and hind-leg of animal facing left; in centre, trunk of tree or palm-frond; and to the right, an unidentified motif, perhaps the flounced skirt of a standing figure.

REGISTRATION No. 5510:29
**Dimensions:** 1.64 x 1.26 x 0.86.
**Reverse:** String-impression.
**Location:** Building 224, Area 316. Floor.
**Description:** Light-grey, irregular fragment with white inclusions. **Obverse:** Small segment of edge of a possible impression, no design visible.

REGISTRATION No. 5510:30
**Dimensions:** 1.6 x 0.95 x 0.93.
**Reverse:** Two parallel string-impressions.
**Location:** Building 224, Area 316 Floor.
**Description:** Light-grey, unbaked, irregular fragment.
**Obverse:** No identifiable motif, finger-print.

REGISTRATION No. 5510:31

**Dimensions:** 2.2 x 0.85 x 1.0.
**Reverse:** String-impression, and possible impression of tip of small, smooth peg.
**Location:** Building 224, Area 316. Floor.
**Description:** Fragment of fine, yellowish clay. One slightly-concave, smooth edge with finger-prints. **Obverse:** Part of lower right segment of design. Standing figure in tiered skirt, upper body and head missing; to the right is a jar with unidentified motifs above and to the right. Similar to 5510:18 (q.v.) and related sealings, but not possible to say if from same seal.

## REGISTRATION No. 5510:32

**Dimensions:** 1.3 x 1.25 x 0.63.
**Reverse:** Worn, possible string-impression.
**Location:** Building 224, Area 316. Floor.
**Description:** Light-grey, poorly preserved fragment. **Obverse:** Part of possible quadruped, above which are the feet and lower skirt of a human figure, with a star motif to his left.

## REGISTRATION No. 5510:33

**Dimensions:** 1.7 x 1.06 x 0.9.
**Reverse:** Possible reed impressions.
**Location:** Building 224, Area 316. Floor.
**Description:** Light-grey, irregular piece of clay, apparently pinched into triangular shape. **Obverse:** Poorly preserved, but appears to show part of horned animal facing right, its head turned back over its shoulder, and a plant motif above its rump.

## REGISTRATION No. 5510:34

**Dimensions:** 1.5 x 1.43 x 0.7.
**Reverse:** Possible knot-impression.
**Location:** Building 224, Area 316. Floor.
**Description:** Light-grey fragment, with one smoothed surface, with a single line, perhaps the edge of a sealing.

## REGISTRATION No. 5510:35

**Dimensions:** 1.42 x 1.5 x 0.95.
**Reverse:** Worn, possible knot-impression.
**Location:** Building 224, Area 316. Floor.
**Description:** Light-grey, poorly preserved fragment. Small area of smoothed edge with two triangular indentations.
**Obverse:** Badly worn figure of animal facing left, above the feet and lower skirt of a human figure facing right.

## REGISTRATION No. 5510:36

**Dimensions:** 1.3 x 0.73 x 0.63.
**Reverse:** One fine string-impression.
**Location:** Building 224, Area 316. Floor.
**Description:** Light-grey clay, unbaked, semicircular fragment, with an arc of smoothed edge, and tiny segment of seal impression, with illegible motifs. Part of same sealing as 5510:23.

## REGISTRATION No. 5510:37

**Dimensions:** 1.0 x 0.5 x 0.4.
**Reverse:** Surface missing.
**Location:** Building 224, Area 316. Floor.
**Description:** Light-grey fragment. One convex surface with possible impression of parallel lines.

## REGISTRATION No. 5510:38
See 5510:24.

## REGISTRATION No. 5510:39

**Dimensions:** 1.0 x 0.98 x 0.95.
**Reverse:** Possible string-impression.
**Location:** Building 224, Area 316. Floor.
**Description:** Yellowish clay fragment, roughly cone-shaped, with a chip off the apex of the cone. **Obverse:** Irregular lines; possible impression.

## REGISTRATION No. 5510:40
See 5510:24.

## REGISTRATION No. 5510:41
See 5510:24.

## REGISTRATION No. 5510:42
See 5510:24.

## REGISTRATION No. 5510:43
See 5510:24.

## REGISTRATION No. 5510:44

**Dimensions:** 0.7 x 0.8 x 0.46.
**Reverse:** No impression.
**Location:** Building 224, Area 316. Floor.
**Description:** Fragment of light-grey clay. Small, of irregular shape, with very small area of smoothed edge.
**Obverse:** Hem of skirt and pair of feet facing left, with another foot facing right on left edge. Very similar to 5510:18 (q.v.), and related sealings, but not possible to say if from same seal.

## REGISTRATION No. 5510:51
Amalgamated with 5510:24.

## REGISTRATION No. 5510:52

**Dimensions:** 1.57 x 1.46 x 0.65.
**Reverse:** Possible reed or wood impressions, and one doubtful string-impression.
**Location:** Building 224, Area 316. Floor.
**Description:** Fragment of fine, yellowish clay. One quarter of seal impression, with fragment of smoothed edge with finger-print.
**Obverse:** Top left quarter of design. Goose-like bird looking right towards a palm-frond. Below the bird is a horizontal, hatched motif, perhaps the horizontal arm of a cross dividing up the surface of the seal.

## REGISTRATION No. 6003:09

**Dimensions:** 2.1 x 2.05 x 1.35.
**Reverse:** String-impression, originally in centre of bulla(?).
**Location:** Building 63, Area 331. Sand.
**Description:** Perhaps half of a bulla. Very fine, light-grey clay, with rare, tiny, white and light-grey inclusions. Originally ovoid or round. Surviving piece represents one rounded end with smooth exterior surface. No impression.

## REGISTRATION No. 6075:01

Three fragments, two joined.
**Dimensions:** (i/ii) together 1.75 x 0.84 x 0.95. (iii) 2.09 x 1.2 x 0.7.
**Reverse:** (i/ii) String-impression.
**Location:** Building 64, Area 333. Sand.
**Description:** Fine, light-greenish clay.
(i/ii) Fragmentary impressions of the edge of a circular seal.

## REGISTRATION No. 6079:06

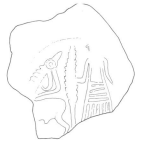

**Dimensions:** 2.5 x 2.22 x 1.29.
**Reverse:** Knot-impressions.
**Location:** Building 64, Area 306. Occupation.
**Description:** Light-brown, fine clay, with rare white inclusions. Obverse has impression of circular seal, and a damaged human figure, looking left, holding palm-branch to the right, with long-horned animal, facing left, neck outstretched, head thrown back. Finger-prints.

## REGISTRATION No. 6580:06

**Dimensions:** 2.24 x 1.85 x 0.67.
**Reverse:** Parallel striations, possibly reed, and string.
**Location:** Building 60, Area 372. Floor.
**Description:** Pinkish baked clay. Quarter segment of edge with finger-prints. **Design:** A cross with arms outlined by double lines. Two complete arms end in hatched squares. Four single lines radiate from the angles of the arms of the cross, the two complete ones ending in crescents.

## REGISTRATION No. E18:15:05

**Dimensions:** 3.0 x 3.5 x 1.4.
**Reverse:** Two parallel string-impressions, and oblong string-hole, diam. 0.4.
**Location:** Building 14, Area 7. Occupation.
**Description:** Burnt grey clay. About half preserved. Part of smoothed edge. **Obverse:** Upper half of a seal impression, showing on the left the head of a horned animal, facing left. In front of its face is a curved palm-branch or tree. Behind the head, above the animal's back, is a much smaller animal, a male quadruped with ruffed neck, facing left, but with head turned back over its shoulder. Part of another motif is just visible below its hind-legs. Estimated diam. of seal c.2.4.

## REGISTRATION No. F17:75:01

**Dimensions:** 3.1 x 3.0 x 1.1, estimated diam. of seal c.2.2.
**Reverse:** Deep knot-impression.
**Location:** Building 14, Area 12. Floor.
**Description:** Burnt clay. Approximately circular. Part of the edge also has string-marks. **Obverse:** A central, standing figure facing right, holding a long pointed object in front of him, at waist height, and at right angles to his body. He is wearing a hatched skirt, and has an elongated neck and stylised head. There is a rosette to the right of his head. Another is present below the horizontal object. On the left side he holds a badly damaged, inverted, horned animal, which faces right.

## REGISTRATION No. F18:45:21

**Dimensions:** 1.37 x 1.03 x 0.4.
**Reverse:** Smoothed.
**Location:** Building 1, Area 2. Occupation.
**Description:** Roughly triangular piece of fine, pinkish clay. Possible motif on one surface.

## REGISTRATION No. K17:76:03

(ii)

**Dimensions:** (i) 0.58 x 0.26 x 0.74.
(ii) 1.16 x 0.94 x 0.49.
(iii) 2.26 x 1.46 x 1.45.
**Reverse:** (i) String-impression.
(ii) String-impression. (iii) Parallel impressions.
**Location:** Building 5, Area 59. Occupation.
**Description:** Three fragments. Brownish, hard, burnt clay.
(i) Pinched fragment with finger-print on one surface.
(ii) **Obverse:** Impression of circular seal, probably just lower left corner of impression missing. Design forms a rosette. A central circle is surrounded by four others (only three extant). Each of the outer circles is separated from the next by a short line radiating from the centre.
(iii) **Obverse:** A second impression from the same seal as (ii), this time with much of top and left edge preserved as

well as centre. The central circle and two outer ones are present, and three of the radiating lines. Estimated diam. of seal 2.1.

## REGISTRATION No. M16:33:07

**Dimensions:** 1.3 x 0.9 x 0.4.
**Reverse:** Flat surface with faint striations.
**Location:** Building 56, Area 72. Make-up.
**Description:** Fragment of clay sealing in pale-grey clay.
**Obverse:** Part of the left edge of a seal impression, showing a standing, naked, human figure in profile, facing right, with an arm raised. To the right is the head of an animal with ruffed neck and long, swept-back horns, facing left but turning back over its shoulder. The figures are very small, and the carving fine. Style Ib(?).

## REGISTRATION No. P20:02:07

**Dimensions:** 0.82 x 0.8 x 0.3.
**Reverse:** Possible string-impression.
**Location:** Building 101, Area 107. Sand.
**Description:** Small, roughly rectangular fragment of grey ashy clay, faint scratches on one surface.

## REGISTRATION No. P20:02:08

**Dimensions:** 1.0 x 0.7 x 0.2.
**Reverse:** Impression of fine string.
**Location:** Building 101, Area 107. Sand.
**Description:** Hard, pinkish, fired flake, roughly-rectangular, with finely drawn body of animal, facing left, head destroyed, a sun symbol above its back, and a vertical motif to its right.

REGISTRATION No. 1159:05

**Dimensions:** 1.8 x 2.2 x 0.75.
**Reverse:** String-hole, and tubular impression.
**Location:** Building 200, Area 204. Floor.
**Description:** Probably part of token with hemispherical back, originally pierced for suspension.
**Obverse:** Hatched square (4 x 6 squares), with necks of two short-horned animals protruding from top, one looking left and one right. To left is damaged figure of three-toed rampant monster, looking right. Below this a head of animal with long back-swept horns facing left.

REGISTRATION No. 1159:07

**Dimensions:** 1.2 x 2.0 x 0.75.
**Reverse:** Surface largely missing.
**Location:** Building 200, Area 204. Floor.
**Description:** Fragment of possible hemispherical token.
**Obverse:** Head of animal looking right to edge of seal, with back-swept horns, and three-toed foot or hoof raised in front of face. (N.B. not the same design as 1159:05).

REGISTRATION: 2126:01

**Dimensions:** Diam. 1.5, max. height 0.8.
**Reverse:** Convex, with finger-prints and textile impression.
**Location:** Building 57, Area 74. Occupation.
**Description:** Hemispherical piece of grey clay.

**Obverse:** Four stylised, deeply incised, horned heads, possibly of bulls, in rotation, horns facing towards the outer rim. Clay apparently burnt. Faint textile impression. Previously published Woodburn & Crawford 1994, p. 100, Fig. 15, and Crawford 1998b, p. 54, Fig. 1.

REGISTRATION No. 2126:02

**Dimensions:** Diam. 2.15, height 1.3.
**Reverse:** Hemispherical, surface eroded.
**Location:** Building 57, Area 74. Occupation.
**Description:** Dark-grey, burnt clay, button-shaped token, pierced for suspension on a very thin cord.
**Obverse:** No design visible.

REGISTRATION No. 2665:06

**Dimensions:** Diam. 2.05, height 0.84.
**Reverse:** Convex with finger-prints.
**Location:** Building 53, Area 84. Occupation.

**Description:** Slightly-irregular, hemispherical token, of burnt, pinky-grey clay. Complete seal impression, with edge of seal visible in places. **Obverse:** Three concentric circles, each with loops on outer edge: nine on central circle, fourteen or fifteen on the middle one, and on the outer the impression is too shallow to say. From the same seal as 5500:27. Also identical in design to a bifacial example from the Barbar Temple (Beyer 1989, p. 154, No. 284). Two more (unifacial examples) with identical pattern can be seen on display in the Bahrain National Museum, one from Qala'at al-Bahrain, the other of undeclared provenance. A seal from Failaka also has the same distinctive design (Kjaerum 1983, No. 37). Previously published Moon & Killick 1995, Pl. 33g; Crawford 1998b, p. 52, Pl. 2.

## REGISTRATION NO. 5012:06

**Dimensions:** 1.53 x 1.7 x 0.5.
**Reverse:** Convex.
**Location:** House 224, Area 307. Sand.
**Description:** Hemispherical. Unpierced. Fine, hard, red clay. **Obverse:** Very worn impression, showing perhaps two or three standing figures on a boat. Three interlocking circles below 'boat'. Discussed in Crawford 1998b, p. 53.

## REGISTRATION NO. 5176:02

**Dimensions:** 2.3 x 2.4 x 1.05.
**Reverse:** Smooth and convex, with finger-prints, and remains of a transverse hole.
**Location:** Building 220, Area 309. Floor.
**Description:** Light-pink, baked clay. Lower left segment of impression of a large seal, estimated diam. c.2.8. Small section of edge. **Obverse:** On left is a standing, skirted, human figure

with top half missing, facing right. To the right, legs of a male quadruped, facing right. Below, on lower edge, a standing male quadruped with long horns, facing right and looking upwards. Below its head a possible bush.

## REGISTRATION NO. 5196:01

**Dimensions:** Not measured.
**Reverse:** Roughly domed.
**Location:** Building 220, Area 312. Tannur.
**Description:** Sub-oval fragment of fired orange clay, possibly from a token. **Obverse:** Faint parallel lines.

## REGISTRATION NO. 5211:07

**Dimensions:** Length 2.74, width 1.75, thickness 1.1, estimated diam. of seal 1.8.
**Reverse:** Bifacial.
**Location:** Building 220, Area 314. Occupation.
**Description:** Segment of a circular disk. Sandy, light-brown, burnt clay. Side 1: About one-third of circular sealing, from right side of impression. The head and claws of a scorpion, facing down, on rim of seal; below, also around the rim, a second complete scorpion, facing down. To the left, a comb motif, and the curved back of a possible monkey-like creature, broken. Side 2: To the right, a seated monkey-like creature, with arms outstretched towards the skirt of a standing figure in a tiered skirt, damaged. Two different seals appear to have been used to impress this seal. Discussed in Crawford 1998b, p 53.

## REGISTRATION No. 5500:27

**Dimensions:** Diam. 1.85–2.1, height 0.7.
**Reverse:** Hemispherical.
**Location:** Building 224, Area 316. Sand.
**Description:** Hard-baked, red clay. Worn. Large, sub-circular nick taken out of one edge.

**Obverse:** Triple concentric circles with small loops on outer side of each circle. From the same seal as 2665:06 (q.v.). Previously published Killick et al. 1993, p. 3, Fig. 11; also discussed Crawford 1998b, p. 53.

## REGISTRATION No. 6539:01

**Dimensions:** Diam. 2.2–1.9, max. thickness 0.9, min. thickness 0.5.
**Reverse:** Bifacial.
**Location:** Building 60, Area 372. Floor.
**Description:** Oval disk, hard pinkish clay, thicker on one edge than the other. Impressed on either side with different seals, each design virtually a mirror-image of the other. Side 1: An arrow-head, pointing up, inside a square. To the left of the square, a palm-frond. Above and below the square, curved lines, possibly crescents, the lower one upside-down. From the right edge of the square protrude the curved necks of two animals, heads missing. Side 2: The impression is at a diagonal to that on the first side and is a mirror image of it. An arrow-head, pointing down, inside a square. To the left, traces of a palm-frond, this time upside-down. Above and below the square, the same crescents as on the first side. From the right side of the square protrude the curved necks of two animals. The left-hand head is missing. From the same pair of seals as K16:53:02. A unifacial token with the same design was found at Qala'at al-Bahrain (Beyer 1989, p. 154, No. 284), and there is a seal from Failaka with the same design again (Kjaerum 1983, No. 52). Previously published Crawford 1998b, p. 52, Pl. 1.

## REGISTRATION No. 6580:04

**Dimensions:** 2.7 x 2.3 x 0.85, approx. diam. of seal 2.3.
**Reverse:** Slightly-convex, smooth back, with finger-prints, and a probable string-impression on one edge.
**Location:** Building 60, Area 372. Floor.
**Description:** Virtually-complete token. Design: Three standing figures in long, tiered skirts with linked hands. Two figures on the left face left, the third perhaps right. The left figure holds a shield with spikes at the top and bottom to his left. Possible fourth figure to the right. Impression worn.

## REGISTRATION No. F17:78:02

**Dimensions:** Diam. 1.85, height of edge 0.65, thickness of centre 0.3.
**Reverse:** Possibly bifacial.
**Location:** House 14, Area 17. Pit.
**Description:** Broken token. Dark-grey clay, heavily burnt. Half of a circular disk of clay with raised edge, smoothed on outside edge. No trace of an impression.

## REGISTRATION No. K16:53:02

**Dimensions:** Diam. 1.95–2.0, thickness 0.5–0.85.
**Reverse:** Bifacial.
**Location:** Building 51, Area 56. Make-up.
**Description:** Circular piece of brown clay. Both sides have a seal impression; one side of disk thinner than the other. Side 1: Square containing a tanged arrow-head. The remains of two animal necks protrude from the right, a palm-frond to the left. Above the square is a crescent lying on its back. Side 2: Mirror image of the same design. From the same seal as 6539:01 (q.v.). Previously published Crawford 1993, pp. 11 & 12, Fig. 12, and 1998b, p. 58, Pl. 1.